Survive the Modern World

How
to have
MEANINGFUL
Relationships

Emma Power

Hardie Grant

BOOKS

Introduction

When our relationships are firing, our souls sing in alignment. We feel secure and motivated, heart-burstingly happy. But when these connections shift, we can find ourselves disconnected. Distanced, conflicted or blindly wading our way through poor communication battles. Our souls ache in the dark.

We're all born with hearts to love, ears to listen and arms to hug, but we don't arrive Earthside with relationship skills; they need to be learnt and practiced. It's strange that, in a world of life goals and chasing dreams, it's not common to devote time to boosting connections with our nearest and dearest. Imagine what would happen if we poured the same amount of energy that we put into our hobbies or work into our relationships? It's upskilling with the most rewarding upside.

You're about to unearth the foundations for building stronger connections, learn how to lay down boundaries, unleash the power of staying present for your people and discover how to diffuse dreaded conflict bombs. Most importantly, you're about to master the most significant relationship in your life – the one with yourself.

We're going to get deep, soul seeker, and it's going to be meaningful. Prepare for a shift, a shake-up and success because once you start reading, you're setting up yourself – and your relationships – for change.

Ready? Big breath. Let's dive in.

Chapter One

SELF-Love

You've got your own back

It's no accident that this book kicks off with self-love. If you're seeking meaningful relationships, you need to begin with you. Why? Because your relationship with yourself is the longest and most important relationship you will ever have.

The way you think and feel about yourself shapes your life far more than you may realise. In fact, it influences just about *everything* – how you let people treat you, the type of romantic relationship you may be in, the jobs you go for, the pay you accept, your daily mindset, the way you treat yourself. All of this comes back to self-love.

What is self-love?

Imagine this ... You have the best bestie in the world. You know they've got your back. When you need someone, they are there. They are loyal. They're great company and they make you laugh. They comfort, affirm and speak lovingly to you. They care for you and know just what you need. They never compromise your needs. They *get* you.

Self-love is giving all of those things to yourself.

While having a bestie like that would be great, the truth about relationships is that they have ups and downs, they come and go and they're affected by factors beyond your control. When you self-love, you're investing in someone who's here to stay, always.

Some people confuse self-love with narcissism and so shy away from the idea. But there's a clear difference. When someone is narcissistic, their sense of self is incredibly fragile, and they prey on the energy of others to prop themselves up and feed their disorder. It's about as far from self-love as it gets.

Self-love is warmer than self-respect and deeper than self-esteem; it goes further than self-care, is more powerful than self-confidence and beyond self-worth. It contains all of those things, but it's so much more. There's an intimacy that self-love brings that only you can give to yourself. Oscar Wilde described it as 'a lifelong romance'. From a spiritual perspective, self-realisation and self-love go hand in hand. When you begin to recognise who you truly are, you can't help but love what you see.

As you grow in self-love, you'll discover that what you have been seeking from everything around you can actually be found within you. That may seem a bit abstract or far-fetched, but it is my hope that as you take this journey, an inner strength and deep peace will begin to reveal itself to you.

To self-love is to know yourself intimately – and to accept what you see. You don't have to *become* something loveable in order to love yourself. Rather, you will no longer judge any part of yourself as unlovable. Through this process of discovering yourself – even the parts you've been disregarding or avoiding – not only will you come to a place of self-acceptance, but also one of honouring and celebration.

QUIZ

What's your self-love level?

Work through the list below and assign each statement a number on the scale of 1 to 5: 5 is 'I've nailed this!' and 1 is 'This virtually doesn't exist for me'. There's no judgment here. It's almost impossible to make it through life without your self-love taking a hit in some areas. In many ways, lack of self-love is cultural – many of us have spent years being exposed to reasons as to why we shouldn't love ourselves. This quiz will help to identify the areas to take action.

Quiz statements

* You bring intention to the way you live. Rather than letting life just happen to you, you play an active role in the choices you make and the path you take.

* You act on what you need rather than what you want. You have the strength to break old behavioural patterns that have hurt you in the past. Yes, you may want to have sex with your ex, or eat the sugary snack, or do late-night scrolling. Instead, you lovingly steer yourself in a direction that will feel better later.

* You set boundaries like a boss. You're aware of how you spend your emotional, mental and physical energy and you know what's good for you. You can easily draw a line in the sand and set limits or say no to work, relationships or activities that harm or deplete you.

* You practice self-care, nourishing yourself with good food, exercise, time in nature and plenty of sleep. You think of your body as your loving home and are intentional about how you treat it. You neither neglect your health nor obsess over your physical appearance.

* You surround yourself with people who are cheering you on. If they're not, you walk away, take a break and/or limit your time with them. You know that life is too short to spend time with people who try to take away your sunshine.

* You take responsibility for your mistakes but don't beat yourself up. You can find gold in your stuff-ups, recognising that these were the lessons you needed to learn. You have compassion for your humanness and accept imperfections.

* You are aware of the dangers of comparison and you know how to stay in your own lane. When others do well, you are inspired by them or able to celebrate them. It doesn't affect your own self-confidence.

* You have awareness around what you watch, read and scroll because you know this affects your vibe which, in turn, shapes your life. When you zone out, you do so consciously to give yourself a break rather than to feed an addiction.

* Rather than taking pride in how much you do, you take pride in how good you feel. You know that following your joy or having downtime is nothing to be ashamed of. Your version of success comes from an internal feeling, rather than an external accomplishment.

* You speak kindly to yourself. You notice when you slip into self-deprecating thoughts, and you adjust your sails accordingly. You give yourself the self-respect you know you deserve.

* The environments you live, work and spend time in feel good to you. You've tailored your lifestyle to reflect your dreams, desires and passions.

* You receive the pay you deserve for the work you do.

* You never seek permission to be yourself. You've dropped the people-pleasing and appeasing. Worrying about what others think pulls you away from living authentically, and you're no longer prepared to compromise on that.

* You can receive help from others easefully and ask for support when you need it.

* You love the people in your life, but you don't depend on them to bring you happiness. When your relationships come into conflict, you self-regulate to make sure you're not taken on a rollercoaster, and you're not taking their 'stuff' personally.

* You're constantly learning new things about yourself, updating the way you view the world and expanding the way you think. You take time to make contact with your inner world.

* You've stopped using the term 'self-improvement'. You know that the best way to be you doesn't come from striving to be something else, but by removing all the labels that tell you that you aren't enough already.

Score

1–2: This is an area where a lack of self-love is showing up. You can use this as a reference to apply the tools coming up in this chapter.

3 – You have awareness of the areas in which you don't self-love and it's a habit you're beginning to break.

4 – Woohoo! Loving yourself comes pretty easily. You recognise the occasions when you drop out of self-love and make the appropriate adjustments to get back on track.

5 – Love your work! You've mastered this area.

Why don't we love ourselves?

We are constantly bombarded with images of perfection – the perfect lifestyles, bodies and relationships. Media and, even more so, social media can take some of the blame for that. Constantly comparing yourself can certainly put a dent in your self-love tank!

It may also be stemming from early years. Many parents don't realise the deep imprint they leave on their children. You may have had a model of a parent who didn't self-love, or you may have had unachievable expectations placed on you throughout your childhood. And even if your parents did love you deeply, you may have assumed a situation or reaction was due to you being flawed or unloveable. Little people have a tendency to think things are about them even when they're not, and this can leave its mark.

Your self-love deficit may be a result of relationship issues. Bullying, break-ups, unhealthy dynamics. Perhaps the people you surround yourself with are bringing you down.

Finally, we need to acknowledge that the culture we live in makes money off our lack of self-love. The system is designed that way. If we are always searching for something outside of ourselves to fill us up and make us feel like we're worthy and loveable, we will continuously spend money in order to try to fill the void.

It can be helpful to unpack where a lack of self-love stems from, but even if it isn't clear, that doesn't mean you can't heal. Quite often, healing comes naturally from having the opposite experience to the one you're conditioned to expect.

You are allowed
to be both a
MASTERPIECE
and a *work
in progress*
simultaneously *

Sophia Bush

Self-love and relationships

Self-love plays a huge role in our connections with others. The way we treat ourselves and feel about ourselves will be reflected in the quality of our friendships and relationships.

Here are a few ways it can show up in our connections:

Inability to receive love

When we don't self-love, it can be difficult to fully receive love from others. We might be surrounded by wonderful people who pour love into us, but they won't be able to make us feel worthy if we don't perceive those things within ourselves. It's as though our capacity for love is too small to believe it.

We might go so far as to sabotage relationships and push loved ones away. Subconsciously, we may create reasons or find ways to convince them of how unloveable we are. In some cases, this may go as far as destroying a beautiful relationship that has incredible potential, all because we don't love ourselves enough.

Staying in something you shouldn't

A deficit in self-love might manifest in the relationship choices you make and what you choose to tolerate. You may settle for being with someone who doesn't treat you well, or a situation or dynamic that is abusive. Or perhaps you stay in relationships that you know aren't right for you because you believe that's all you deserve or that you won't be able to find anything better.

Hiding the true you

If you lack self-love, you may lack the confidence to admit your preferences, show who you truly are or state your real opinions. Like a chameleon, you change yourself according to the environment you're in. You go along with what other people want and say out of fear that you won't be accepted if you assert yourself. You may find that your relationships lack authenticity because you're not being the true you.

Co-dependency

Perhaps you see another person as your 'other half'. Although it sounds sweet, it's not healthy. If you don't see yourself as whole, you'll always be seeking someone else to complete you.

When you're co-dependent, you also feel responsible for other people's emotional states. You're usually overly vigilant about the other person's needs, to the point of neglecting yourself. When you lose yourself in this way, you also risk losing your intuition and your sense of yourself as an autonomous, independent person on your own unique journey.

You're not a priority

You may find that people in your life don't prioritise you. They may even walk all over you. This is most likely happening because you are not prioritising yourself. You're teaching people how to treat you by how you treat yourself. You are sending out invisible but very real signals and you're setting a standard. Have a think: how high is yours?

PRACTICE

Take another look at the previous list. Do you see any of these dynamics playing out in your current relationships? Is there a dynamic that seems to repeat itself in your connections with people?

Feel-good *and* good-for-you lists

Make two lists. One will be a list of all the things that make you feel good – soft, relaxed, peaceful, filled-up. This could be a massage, reading on the couch, sleeping in, spending time with friends. The other will be a list of things that are good for you. It could be exercise, a yoga class, morning meditation or eating a big salad.

Be specific. Rather than adding 'get more sleep', write 'Be in bed by 9.30 pm'. If you need less caffeine, you might say, 'Stick to one cup of coffee per day'. If it helps you to write your lists, also ask yourself:

* What do I feel deprived of?
* What do I need less of?

Now, go back and take a look at your self-love level quiz results. For each statement that you scored lower on, add something to your list. Perhaps you scored a 1 or 2 on the way you speak to yourself, so choose a loving affirmation that you will repeat to yourself at least ten times throughout the day. Add this to the good-for-you list.

 # PRACTICE

30-day challenge

For a month, *every day*, choose to do at least one thing from each list. Pick the things you know you need most in the moment. So although you may want to see your friends for a night out, what you might need is to lay in the bath. You may find these lists lengthen as you get clearer on what you need and want to feel nourished.

Start of the day

When you see yourself in the mirror, look into your eyes and say the following simple statement: 'I love you.' Sounds simple, doesn't it? Some people really love this practice. But for most, this tiny exercise will feel embarrassing, even excruciating. If that's the case, it's even more important that you do it.

End of the day

The moments just before you drift off to sleep are a powerful time for the subconscious mind. Place a hand on your heart and offer yourself a loving message, something you would want to hear from a loved one. The message I've been using for years is super simple. I say, 'Goodnight, beautiful. I love you.' We often take our final thoughts before sleep into our dreams; make sure it's a good one.

Self-love as practice

So what does self-love *look* like? What does it feel like to you? Some might think self-love is a massage, or a bath, or a walk on the beach. Although these things feel nice, doing them occasionally isn't going to fundamentally change things. True self-love won't come from a one-off feel-good moment. Self-love is a practice, a journey rather than a destination. It's a lifelong commitment to yourself.

It's like you're dating yourself and, like any relationship, it takes habitual re-commitment, again and again. These practices need to be repeated so that they become a way of being. Eventually, it will become your default to take care of your precious self. You will automatically speak to yourself with care, and you won't think twice about nurturing yourself with healthy foods. It will feel natural to preserve your energy, stand up for yourself, follow what lights you up, and spend time with people who genuinely care for you. When you self-love, you'll no longer abandon yourself when the going gets tough, through numbing out or caving in. You'll be right there, by your own side, holding yourself through and cheering yourself on.

Self-love is not selfish

All these exercises may feel unusual at first. They are extremely intimate, and not many of us are used to knowing ourselves well enough to feel okay with that.

We romanticise the idea of having time for ourselves or doing the things we love, but most people's adrenals are running so high that it can be a challenge to relax into the love of this month. It may take time to be okay with feeling good. You may feel like you need to explain to the people around you why you deserve it. That's the lack of self-love talking.

Here's why you should stick with it.

When you're feeling good, full to the brim, there's a spring in your step and you feel lit-up. You've tapped into a source of flowing abundance (your self-love tank) and there's plenty to go around, so you can't help but pour that goodness into the people you meet. Your energy will be infectious; the people around you will feel energised and better about themselves. You'll be a glowing gift of self-love.

It's not the main reason to self-love, but it's a great effect. The people who can handle the new you, the *real* you, will benefit. So if you want to give back, start first with filling your cup so you've got something worth giving.

Heartfelt check-in

Put a reminder in your phone now, then open this chapter up in a month and re-do the quiz. See where your answers have changed for the better. If you've followed the program, your numbers will certainly be inching, if not leaping, up the scale.

To depend on the EXTERNAL has our *JOY* and HAPPINESS riding on a variable ✳

Stay open to self-love

The quiz helps identify the areas to work on and the exercises to create a new way of living, but essentially, the most important thing here is your mindset. For self-love to truly work, you'll need to be willing; willing to let go of the need for validation, willing to accept and honour all of who you are, willing to be real. You have the choice, every day, to show up.

Are you willing to risk being you? To strip yourself bare, to wipe the slate clean of the shoulds and shouldn'ts you've been told and are holding onto. To ask, 'who am I without all of that?'

The stakes are high, because you'll lose who you've been pretending to be and so will the people around you. That might feel initially uncomfortable, but let's be real; it hasn't exactly been feeling good to try to fit into an image anyway, right?

As you move forward, you'll begin to find you are more loving and connected to you. There will be less urgency for the approval of others. You'll stop explaining yourself and simply start *being* yourself. You'll stop abandoning any aspect of who you are. Eventually, none of this will take conscious practice. It will simply be your new normal.

The phrase 'to be full of yourself' will take on new meaning. Before this, you were part you and part everyone else. Now, you are whole and complete. And self-love looks really, really good on you.

Chapter Two

THE Perfection MYTH

Moving past comparisons and managing expectations

When it comes to relationships, it's tempting to think that other people have perfected the art of connection. It's easy to believe that you're the only one who experiences conflict, frustration, fragmentation, distance and a lack of intimacy. This can feel isolating, disappointing and like you've failed somehow. It's a lonely place to be – thinking that everyone else has perfect lives and relationships while you're wondering what went wrong with yours. It can also place pressure on your relationships, creating the opposite effect of what you're hoping to achieve.

Fairytales, movies, media and social media all play a role in this. We are constantly exposed to endless images of filtered perfection, perfectly curated to make you feel ... imperfect. Lacking. Less than. But when we really look, we find that what we're seeing is mostly a lack of authenticity. Of course, most people aren't going to be in the middle of a slinging match and stop to take a selfie so they can share authentically on the 'gram, so when we're scrolling through other people's lives, we need to keep in mind that we're only seeing a fragment of what's really going on. A staged public performance of sorts.

We also have to contend with the perfection myth in our own minds. Whether it's the image of a perfect wedding and marriage, a perfect parent or sibling, or the perfect best friend, most of us have spent our lives building up ideas of what things should look like, creating unattainable images that will leave us feeling less-than in ourselves and hyper-critical of others. The truth is that we never arrive at the perfect anything. Life is a process and an ongoing journey. Striving for perfection will only hinder our progress and slow us right down.

Trying to be perfect for others stops us from being authentic and expecting perfection puts your loved ones in a pressure cooker. Letting go of the expectation of perfection in relationships makes us far more likely to be moving in a direction of love, harmony and intimacy.

I'm not suggesting you let go of your standards. There's nothing more empowering than striving for quality! Research by psychology professor Donald Baucom found that people who have higher standards for their relationships also reported higher levels of satisfaction with those relationships, so realistic expectations are a must. And now that we're self-lovers, we know that's what we deserve, so although you don't believe in perfect, you should believe in happy, harmonious, top-quality connections.

Knowing how to create these quality connections is your gold dust here. It takes skill and, let's face it, most of us weren't born with those foundations. But each of us can become more proficient for our people. We can learn how to create a better version of the way things are now, and improve on how we've been functioning and what we've been experiencing.

However, you will need to do the work and draw on your inner strength. A healthy relationship is not always easy, and it's not conflict-free. There will be triggers and trauma, communication breakdowns and hurt. Be prepared to still have bad days and tricky phases. You'll make mistakes and so will they. This is where you'll grow through what you go through. Armed with the right skillset, you'll be able to resolve some of the problems in your relationships, prevent conflict, and have the mindset to know when and how to manage the differences. And like any learnt skill, it will eventually become second nature.

 # PRACTICE

Settle in with a cup of tea and get your phone out. It's time to get ruthlessly honest about who you follow on social media.

Notice how you feel when you look at the accounts you're following.
* Who are the people who uplift, inspire or bring you joy?
* Which voices feel authentic, offer teachings or promote a cause that you resonate with?
* And which accounts leave you empty, icky or self-doubting?

If you find yourself looking at images that have you comparing, feeling inadequate or looking sideways at your partner thinking *I wish you were more like this*, it's time to unfollow.

Follow accounts that you find yourself commenting on and liking. Let your feeds be a wellspring that puts a smile on your face and brings joy to your heart. The kind of people who you would want to be friends with in real life.

Once every three months, repeat this exercise. As you take back control of what you see, you'll find yourself liberated and empowered. It's easy to forget we have a choice about what we see and what we ignore. So get real and start unfollowing. Your mental health – and your real-life relationships – will thank you for it.

You don't have to be **PERFECT** to create *healthy love,* and neither do your loved ones. You just have to be **WILLING**. *Showing up* is the biggest step

Chapter Three

Building

BLOCKS

Solid foundations
for thriving relationships

In the previous chapter, I suggested you drop the expectation for perfection in your relationships. But I also said you should have high standards. So how do we know where that sweet spot lies?

Meet the building blocks. These eight steps help you to lay the foundations for healthy relationships. They're the ingredients to create connections that will shift you into a new paradigm of relating. Below is a guide on what to expect, what you deserve and what is fair for others to ask of you. It's best to slow down and spend some time on these. Dog-ear the pages because you'll likely be returning as you grow along your journey.

A healthy relationship won't always be a perfect one. But the highs will outweigh the lows. The pieces will be in place for connections that are strong, loving, meaningful and real.

Not perfect, but pretty damn good.

Building Block One: Kindness

It's cool to be kind, but what does kindness really mean? While it's often associated with being a 'good person', it's important to understand that true kindness is never for show or approval. Kindness is a way of being – a mindset that continues even when no one is there to give you brownie points. It's removing any filter of 'What's in it for me?' and instead asking, 'How can I fill

* True **INDEPENDENCE** means *consciously* maintaining your **AUTONOMY** while still loving *fully*

# PRACTICE

Try the following mantra on for size. State it out loud or silently to yourself.

I deserve kindness.

How did that feel?

_____

Next, consider what kindness looks like to you
and how it shows up in your life.
For me, kindness from another looks like ...

_____

_____

What does kindness look like when you offer it to yourself?
Being kind to myself looks like ...

_____

_____

Now, it's time to consider if there's someone you could be
offering more kindness to.

_____ *deserves my support.*

Let's get specific on ways you could action that.
This would look like ...

_____

_____

them up, meet their needs, back their dreams, go gently with their insecurities and support their plans?'

Kindness chooses to not say a clever one-liner that will get them right where it hurts. It errs on the side of trusting another person's intentions, even when the ego wants to point the finger and name names. This doesn't mean we don't get hurt or that we're never angry, but kindness integrates love and care in responding to those difficult conversations.

Self-love and kindness walk hand in hand. Self-love is one of the kindest actions you can take. Because when *you* feel good, kindness comes easily. You smile at a stranger, leave a bigger tip, help someone with their groceries or offer your assistance or care more readily.

Never confuse kindness with being self-sacrificial to the point of it being detrimental to you, or you'll be coming from a place of should. Under those circumstances, your kindness can't be genuine. So, give where you can give and show yourself kindness by knowing and respecting when you can't.

When a culture of kindness is built into a relationship, you look out for each other. Kindness is catching, so when someone knows you've got them, they are likely to be there for you too. You've established a beautiful cycle, a space in which it's safe to be generous.

We are all born with different levels of kindness, but if we are conscious of it, it is a trait that can grow and a behaviour that can be cultivated. And when this happens, things change.

Building Block Two: Loyalty

Loyalty has your back. When it exists in relationships, you can be sure your loved ones will hold you in a space of integrity, when you're with them and when you're not. You know their actions will honour your relationship.

Our inbuilt survival psychology naturally assesses our safety in all situations. Within our relationships, we seek to gather proof that our loved ones can be trusted – or not. This process happens as we observe their actions to see if they withstand tests of trust. If they prove themselves – as only time will tell – we start to relax into a safety net within the connection.

Loyalty is not one-size-fits-all. It's as unique as each relationship. What one person perceives as loyal may be different to another. Take a client of mine, for example. He has no qualms about his girlfriend flirting with other people, but he feels she betrays his loyalty when she doesn't honour her promises and shows up late to their dates.

I also have a friend who considers himself incredibly loyal to his partner. But when his mother talks down to his wife, he says nothing. He remains silent because he's terrified of his mother. His wife sees this as a betrayal of loyalty.

So in conscious relationships it's important to ask, 'What does loyalty look like in our relationship?' and 'What agreements do we commit to honouring?' Sometimes we won't know the answers until trust has been broken, and we realise what is important because what happened didn't feel right. But just because trust is broken doesn't mean it can't be re-established. Some of the strongest relationships are those that survive a betrayal and grow through it. Boundaries become more firmly defined which, in turn, creates clarity and safety.

 # PRACTICE

State the mantra out loud or silently to yourself.
I deserve to feel chosen.

How did that feel?

_____

Next, consider what loyalty looks like for you
and how it shows up in your life.
For me, loyalty from another looks like ...

_____

_____

What does loyalty look like when you offer it to yourself?
Being loyal to myself looks like ...

_____

_____

Now, it's time to consider if there's someone you could be
offering more loyalty to.

This person deserves my loyalty.

Get specific on ways you could action that.

This would look like ...

_____

_____

# PRACTICE

State the mantra out loud or silently to yourself.
I deserve to feel supported.

How did that feel?

_____

Next, consider what support looks like to you
and how it shows up in your life.
For me, support from another looks like ...

_____

_____

What does it look like when you offer yourself support?
Supporting myself looks like...

_____

_____

Now, it's time to consider if there's someone you could
be offering more support to.

This person deserves my support.

Get specific on ways you could action that.

This would look like ...

_____

_____

A relationship culture of loyalty and security is cultivated by both sides, the person earning trust and the one giving it. It is common, especially if you've been betrayed before, to be on the lookout for betrayal – to the point of finding it where it doesn't exist. If this is the case, the stories you are telling yourself may sabotage your new connections, or even create the very thing you're hoping to avoid. Recognise that your fears can cloud perspective and cause you to overreact to a loved one's words or actions. You may be responding to a past experience that isn't reflective of the present. The best loyalty is born beyond commitment. It comes from the feeling you are chosen without any obligation. It says, 'I choose you' over again. Our relationships deserve that reassurance.

Building Block Three: Support

Support is on-the-ground action. It's not thinking of someone, it's *doing* something. While our relationships are ideally a two-way street, rarely does that look like a 50/50 split. There will be times where we need to roll up our sleeves, get right in and help our loved ones out.

Support considers, 'What is the most practical way I can help here?' and 'What are the ways that I can best be of service?'

While often well-intentioned, saying to someone 'Let me know if there's anything I can do to help' is a very unhelpful statement. We might be tempted to use it to feel like we've done something even when, really, we've done nothing. When someone needs support, it's not always easy for them to make their requests known. Choose to support the person first by taking away the chore of finding chores. If you're offering yourself, come up with a list of things you could do, then ask them to choose. In doing so, you vclarify the level of support you're available to offer, and you make it easier for them to accept your help.

Relationships hit a new level of depth and meaning when we show up in the hard times. True character is revealed when we are asked to sacrifice something in order to be there for someone. It fosters a knowing and a new depth. On the other end of the transaction, it's important that support is acknowledged and not expected. Never become complacent in your expectation that the other will give. If your mum has made you dinner, give her your appreciation. A little gesture from you may mean the world.

Building Block Four: Respect

When we respect another, we see them as an equal. That may seem obvious, but many relationships have power imbalances that infiltrate a connection and create an underlying toxicity.

Respect is found in the way we allow for ideas, preferences and opinions, even if they're different from our own. It's in our tone of voice and the way we deliver our sentences. If contempt, criticism, sarcasm, belligerence, mocking or disregard have entered the space, respect is no longer present. In some relationships, it might mark the beginning of the end but, at the very least, it's a recipe for an unhappy connection.

It may take vigilant awareness and raw honesty to see the ways in which we're disrespecting others. This often happens unconsciously in the child/parent relationship, where there is an expectation to 'respect your parent' but the same regard is not returned.

When we respect, we honour another's personhood, regardless of age, gender, background, culture, status or appearance. And that will be felt.

 # PRACTICE

State the mantra out loud or silently to yourself.

I deserve to feel respected.

How did that feel?

_____

Next, consider what respect looks like to you
and how it shows up in your life.

For me, respect from another looks like …

_____

_____

What does it look like when you give yourself respect?

I can show myself respect by …

_____

_____

Now, it's time to consider if there's someone you could
be offering more respect to.

This person deserves my respect.

Get specific on ways you could action that.

This would look like …

_____

_____

PRACTICE

State the mantra out loud or silently to yourself.
I deserve to receive grace.

How did that feel?

_____

Next, consider what grace looks like to you
and how it shows up in your life.
For me, grace from another looks like ...

_____

_____

What does it look like when you offer yourself grace?
I can give myself grace by ...

_____

_____

Now, it's time to consider if there's someone you could
be offering more grace to.

This person deserves grace from me.

Get specific on ways you could action that.

This would look like ...

_____

_____

Building Block Five: Grace

It's easy to accept your loved ones when they're kicking relationship goals, but what happens when they're not? What happens when their other, less-than-perfect, self shows up?

Grace recognises that we – *all* of us – are somewhat imperfect in our behaviours, decisions and actions. Yes, we have our moments when our highest self shines bright, but there are also plenty of moments when it doesn't. Grace accommodates this and allows for humanity.

Grace is given consciously: you're not being a pushover or putting up with bad behaviour. You are making an empowered decision to go easy on someone. It's a gift given, as opposed to a reward earned. It's choosing to be patient with somebody's journey.

How do we know when to give grace? Basically, if it's not a dealbreaker and it doesn't cross your personal boundary, work around it and let it go. If you're constantly sweating the small stuff, you cast a negative light over the relationship and create a damaging dynamic.

Grace is also malleable. There may be times you offer it when you normally wouldn't, based on what a person is going through.

A friend offered me a helpful analogy around grace. She said, 'Think about your dog. When he's naughty, you don't spend energy making him feel bad for his actions. You move on quickly.' Why are we harder on our human relationships? Mistakes are inevitable; the question is how we respond to them.

It may require you to overlook the pile of clothes on the floor ... again. And it may ask you to let them off the hook when they forget your anniversary, or perhaps let go of your righteous position in an argument and agree to disagree.

If you're the one on the giving end of grace, it's only a matter of time before you'll need to receive it. Ask yourself if you would want to be lectured about your shortcomings or reminded

constantly of how you failed? We're not perfect. Sometimes grace –
the giving and the receiving – can be the perfect break we need.

Building Block Six: Independence

Independence supports – and celebrates – the individual. It creates
the mindset where a relationship isn't there to bring happiness or
fill a gap but is a platform for mutual evolution and love. It honours
our differences, offers freedom and encourages self-expression.
Rather than trying to micro-manage or control a loved one, we
support their journey.

Independence encourages time alone for personal reflection and
values growth instead of fearing change. It encourages our loved
ones to live their own life, even if that results in them choosing a
course that isn't aligned with our desires.

Independence does not mean a lack of investment. If you're
thinking, 'I've nailed this building block! Because I don't need
anyone', then you may be deluding yourself. You've likely stepped
out of the game and shut down your heart.

True independence means consciously maintaining your
autonomy while *still loving fully*. You've got both hands on the
table and you're entirely committed, and it's this commitment to
the relationship that has you committed also to yourself. In the
healthiest relationships, whole and complete individuals come
together to create a third entity – the relationship itself. From this
place, both people actively nurture the connection.

To be clear: you don't do your own thing so you can bail on the
current situation. You do your own thing to ensure the health of
your relationship, and you honour your loved ones when they do
the same. This removes the pressure to be responsible for each
other's state of being and helps us to navigate our way back to
where the deepest source of love exists – within.

 # PRACTICE

State the mantra out loud or silently to yourself.
I can be completely committed while also independent.

How did that feel?

_____

Next, consider what independence looks like for you
and how it shows up in your life.
For me, independence looks like …

_____

_____

Now, it's time to consider if there's someone who could
benefit from you supporting their independence.

I am safe to encourage _____ to be independent from me.

Get specific on ways you could action that.

This would look like …

_____

_____

Building Block Seven: Transfiguration

Transfiguration takes us to the core. It is the practice of seeing someone or something as divine, shining with the essence of inner beauty. Try to witness the world around you, and the people in your life, through this lens.

There are two zones for this state. First is automatic transfiguration. When we experience transfiguration in this way, it's a state of being that envelops us. Time stands still as we bear witness to the glory of another's innate radiance and the depths of their true self.

The American Trappist monk Thomas Merton shares his experience of this in his book *Conjectures of a Guilty Bystander*: 'Then it was as if I suddenly saw the secret beauty of their hearts, the depths of their hearts where neither sin nor desire nor self-knowledge can reach, the core of their reality, the person that each one is in God's eyes. If only they could all see themselves as they really are. If only we could see each other that way all the time. There would be no more war, no more hatred, no more cruelty, no more greed ... But this cannot be seen, only believed and "understood" by a peculiar gift.'

Your consciousness is the lens through which you view all of existence. When a person reaches a certain level of awareness, they can still see people's various traits, mistakes and quirks but, beyond those things, they are capable of profoundly recognising and bearing witness to another's pure essence. Those of us who are a little less than enlightened can still have a spontaneous experience of automatic transfiguration. Like the times when a mother witnesses her baby and her heart expands so wide, everything disappears in the presence of absolute perfection. Or perhaps you have a moment where you look at a friend or partner and you easily see them glowing as the best version of themselves. However, most of us can't hold onto this frame of mind for very long or very often.

# PRACTICE

State the mantra out loud or silently to yourself.

I deserve to be seen through a lens of love.

How did that feel?

_____

Next, consider what transfiguration looks like to you
and how it shows up in your life.

For me, transfiguration from another looks like ...

_____

_____

What does it look like when you see yourself through a lens of love?

Transfiguring myself looks like ...

_____

_____

Now, it's time to consider if there's a relationship in which you could be
practicing transfiguration more often.

This person deserves to be transfigured by me.

Get specific on ways you could action that.

This would look like ...

_____

_____

Which is when we come to what I define as conscious transfiguration. This is a choice, a practice. When we consciously transfigure a person, we intentionally bring our attention to focus on their essence. This is easy at the beginning of a relationship but, as time goes on, we can start to forget. As we continue to practice conscious transfiguration, it will, like muscle memory, connect us more easily to the heart space. When the path to the heart becomes a well-worn track, we are more likely to have spontaneous experiences of transfiguration as we have cultivated a tendency to lean towards love. Our daily filter becomes that bit more golden.

When love becomes our default, our relationships transform. We assume the best, and when we do, we amplify the best in those around us. Think about how you feel when someone thinks highly of you: you are more likely to step up to the plate. When we are transfigured by another, we are transfigured into a more real version of ourselves. And what a gift that is.

Just like grace, to consciously transfigure is not to offer excuses for bad behaviour. You can transfigure someone while having boundaries, self-loving, and even while leaving a relationship. This is not about deluding yourself into seeing someone's potential or wishfully thinking your way into the relationship you want. Conscious transfiguration is akin to admiration, appreciation and affirmation. Rather than hoping someone turns into something, you're acknowledging what is already there.

Now, let's explore a less pleasant aspect of this teaching: de-transfiguration.

When we de-transfigure someone, we are charging up a negative perspective of the person and the relationship. Not only have we lost sight of their innate beauty, we have fixated upon their less-than-savoury traits. This creates a slippery slope and we can't stop viewing their behaviour through a negative lens. The relationship inevitably deteriorates. We'll take a closer look at how this occurs, and what we can do to counter it, in an upcoming chapter that explores why loving relationships break down.

If only they could all see themselves as they *REALLY ARE*. If only we could see each other that way **ALL THE TIME.** There would be no more war, no more hatred, no more cruelty, no more greed

Thomas Merton

Some would suggest that to transfigure is to witness a change in another's appearance. Rather than a morphing, however, it's actually a shedding. It's a state of consciousness that can penetrate through layers of fear, insecurity, attachment and ego to the essence of what lies within. One of the reasons it is so easy to witness this in a baby is because a baby has yet to develop all of these layers – they are completely unconditioned. It is in the process of ageing that we accumulate our many masks and develop our ego self. How amazing it is to look into the eyes of a little one and see such purity! Part of the reason people want to hold babies is to be that little bit closer to this state of presentness.

Building Block Eight: Love

What is love, actually? A lot of things are labelled as 'love' – co-dependency, enmeshment, infatuation, comfort ... the list goes on. Often, what we are calling love is conditional on how a person *makes us feel*. Which isn't really love, because that's all about us.

Love is a radical heartfelt acceptance of our loved ones. Knowing them, accepting them. They don't need to prove themselves nor meet our expectations. We simply love them for them. The purest love is a present state. It's not holding an account of the past or projecting into the future. It sits in the now, simply as it is. We hold this state for others while simultaneously holding this state for ourselves. And therein lies the key.

So much of the confusion around love happens when we rely on the other to love us back. In letting go of that requirement, we're not denying ourselves or being self-sacrificial; we simply take the onus off the relationship to be something specific or look a certain way. We place responsibility on ourselves to bring a sense of completion, knowing that we are already whole as we are. In doing so, we are so full to the brim that we fill all our own gaps, and from this place of

PRACTICE

State the mantra out loud or silently to yourself.
I deserve to feel loved and accepted.

How did that feel?

_____

Next, consider what love and acceptance looks like to you,
and how it shows up in your life.
For me, love and acceptance from another looks like ...

_____

_____

What would it look like when you offer yourself love and acceptance?
Giving myself love and acceptance looks like ...

_____

_____

Now, it's time to consider if there's someone you could be
offering more love and acceptance to.
This person deserves to feel loved and accepted by me.

Get specific on ways you could action that.

This would look like ...

_____

_____

fullness, we overflow in love for those around us. Simply pouring out love because we've discovered an abundant source and we know the secret – there's more than enough to go around.

Loving in this way doesn't ask that we let go of our aspirations or our standards. It simply suggests that we shift our focus away from seeking love outside of ourselves. Which is not always easy. And which is why I say love is a practice.

Many of us are afraid to be our true selves out of a fear of losing love. We hide aspects or pieces of ourselves that we deem to be less than perfect so someone (or many people) will love us. The irony here, of course, is that isn't love, because what the other person is loving is an image we've crafted and sold them. What we're afraid to lose isn't the real thing anyway.

Loving truly and purely has us open up when we want to shut down. It has us leaning in when every part of us wants to run. When we practice loving like this, we can disagree while still remaining connected. It asks us to show our hearts and open to love in every new moment, even when it's hard.

Our building blocks empower us to become conscious in our relationships. We no longer accept that our connections are destined to remain the way they are. We step it up. We actively unlearn old patterns and relearn new ways. We grow individually while still staying connected. We accept the challenges and stay aware of the lessons.

Once your blocks are in place, they become the strong foundations to help you conquer relationship storms, create balance and connect deeply. Now that's a life worth building.

PRACTICE

Put a reminder in your phone right now for a month from today.
When the time comes, re-read this list of building blocks
and consider how you've grown.

_____

_____

_____

_____

_____

_____

Chapter Four

MEANINGFUL

Connections

Get deep, get real

Humans are wired for connection. Just like food, water and shelter, our brain considers our social networks an essential aspect of survival. In antiquity, this was certainly the case – without our tribe, we couldn't survive. Although we're technically more self-sufficient these days, we are still social creatures, driven to stay connected by a force beyond cognitive thought. We don't just miss our people; our brain tells us we *need* our people. So when we're not connecting, something doesn't feel right.

In her book, *The Top Five Regrets of the Dying*, Bronnie Ware offers us the profound insights she received from the people she cared for in their final stages of life. She found that the number one regret they had was not showing up in their relationships. 'It all comes down to love and relationships in the end,' she writes. 'That is all that remains in the final weeks, love and relationships.'

That's a pretty strong motivation for us to delve deeper and invest in the relationships that matter to us, starting today. When our connections are of higher quality, our life is of a higher quality. The good news is that those full-to-the-brim, heart-warming interactions don't have to be random or occasional. There are ways to improve your odds of more fulfilled connections, if you're willing to get the ball rolling. Ready to get started?

Be intentional

It's common to be close with people without *really* knowing them; to feel like familiar strangers. Does this sound familiar? If this is the case, catching up with someone can feel a bit empty.

Instead of accepting business as usual, go into your interactions with the intention of getting a bit deeper. Make it a goal to have an experience in the exchange that feels like it dove below the surface. If we don't do this with intention and awareness, we can often end up repeating the same surface-level interactions over and over.

Understand the impact of technology on your connections

We live in a world where we seem more connected than ever, with computers and smartphones almost ubiquitous. But while we may appear to be in touch with each other, many of us aren't authentically connecting. It's no coincidence that our levels of loneliness have skyrocketed in the same time period we've replaced real-life conversations and interactions with digital encounters.

Although there's no doubt that the world of technology has opened up incredible opportunities to meet like-minded people, there's a reason we need face-to-face interaction with other humans. In-person contact creates a level of intimacy and emotional loyalty that we're less likely to experience from behind a screen. These real-life connections allow us to understand and know each other more authentically. There's a certain type of exposure that happens when we are in real-time, in a real place, having a live exchange. Think about how much better it feels to get a kiss and a hug rather than receiving a texted *xo*.

Digital technology also offers us unprecedented opportunities to create masks to hide behind. We can manipulate the images of self to create a false appearance and lifestyle. The gap between the truth of our reality and how it appears has never been greater. It's easy to confuse followers with friends, and it's common to go for a hit of screen connection rather than reaching out for a real-life encounter, which makes it more important than ever that we become intentional in our connections.

Ask yourself:

* Do you find yourself reaching for your phone to fill yourself up?
* Are you feeling lonely?

Be vulnerable and authentic

Commit to being real AF. As humans, we simultaneously crave to be seen for who we truly are while feeling terrified of the exposure. People who aren't authentic in their relationships are usually afraid that they will be judged, left or loved less if others know who they truly are. As a result, we put on masks and happy faces that prevent us from having true depth in our connections. When we receive affirmation for the persona we've created, it gives us even further reinforcement to continue to use it. Again, the irony is that we're not being truly loved if the person who 'loves' us doesn't actually *know* us.

Being vulnerable and authentic gets us straight to the core. It's the antidote to perfectionism. So, how can you peel back your layers? Lean into your self-love. Stop needing to impress. Stop needing to prove yourself. Be transparent. Let people see you are prepared to be real.

This isn't as easy as it sounds; most of us have spent years crafting and maintaining an image of ourselves. However, if you

 # PRACTICE

If you answered yes to either of the questions on the previous page, it's time to reach out. Make a call and create a date with someone. It might be a friend you haven't seen in a while, or someone who seems lonely and in need of contact themselves. This might feel like a scary step but remember that the vast majority of us need more real-life contact. Be the brave one: take the first step and reach out.

 # PRACTICE

Being Honest

✳ Next time someone asks, 'How are you?' answer honestly without using the word 'good'. How are you, *really*? Having a tough day? Feeling frustrated, overwhelmed? Perhaps you're feeling grateful, excited or bored. Be completely honest and observe what happens as a result.

✳ Share something with someone you've never shared before.

keep applying your self-love lessons from the first chapter, it will begin to come more naturally. When your validation comes from within, you can relax and allow yourself to show your true you.

There are many people who have never seen their friends without makeup on. Never seen their partner cry after a big loss. Never knew their family member was suffering from a mental illness. Had never heard the fears, desires and dreams of their parents. These are the relationships we consider our closest yet, sometimes, we don't really know someone well at all. Relationships like this can only last so long. And if they do endure, they lack true depth. When authenticity exists, it gives you permission to be all of who you are without having to hide yourself. Yes, this is vulnerable and incredibly intimate, but it's what gives our relationships a depth and strength.

You know that feeling when you travel and meet someone and you feel like you've known them forever? You feel closer to them than some of the people you've known for years? That's because travelling has you running on a different operating system. You throw caution to the wind because your time frames are shorter. You're away from the familiar, and you have nothing to lose, so you share yourself in ways you wouldn't usually, and your new travel friend does the same.

Authentic relating has us risking being real like that in our everyday lives. It's honest and raw. It's owning our quirks, braving our differences, stating our preferences and exposing our less shiny qualities. We can stop holding it all together and just *be*. In doing this, we give others permission to do the same.

Ask yourself:

* Which relationships do you put masks on for?
* What don't your loved ones know about you?
* Do you feel like you truly know your loved ones or do you feel like familiar strangers?

Quality isn't always comfortable

Don't avoid the difficult conversations. Our happiest connections are the ones in which we are being our authentic selves, even if it causes some discomfort along the way. Paradoxically, this discomfort creates a level of safety in our relationships. We can relax in the knowledge that any bumps along the way will be addressed.

It's okay to ask your parents about your childhood. It's okay to ask them about theirs. It's okay to talk about heartbreak. It's okay to let someone know that they've hurt you, or that you need some space. It's okay to create boundaries in your interactions, and it's okay to tell someone you're struggling with your mental health. Loss, love, pain … this is all of what makes us human.

Avoiding hard conversations means avoiding meaning and having an inauthentic experience. In meaningful relationships, it's important that we learn to become comfortable with uncomfortable emotions.

This may be new territory for some of you but don't worry, you are not on your own. In later chapters, we'll look at boundaries and conflict resolution to help guide you to proceed with caution and express yourself in a way that is more likely to land well. For now, know that a good rule of thumb is that when you feel like you want to run or a conversation feels 'too hard', stay open to the idea of leaning into the challenge.

It's also important to recognise that conversational discomfort and avoidance don't always come from a fear of conflict – sometimes, it's born out of a fear of intimacy. Some of the hardest conversations are the loving ones. Someone was describing his mother to me, and he got tears in his eyes when saying how much he loved her. 'Tell her!' I said. 'Nawwww,' he replied. It's likely she might never know how he feels about her and that is such a missed opportunity, one that he may eventually regret.

It's important that we offer assurance and tell our loved ones how important they are to us. According to John Grey, PhD research psychologist and author of *Five-Minute Relationship Repair*, each of us has a subconscious survival system in our brain that is constantly evaluating how secure we feel in our relationships. He says that unspoken questions like, 'Do I matter to you?' and 'Do you accept me as I am?' are always running through our minds, whether we are conscious of them or not. Assurance is therefore crucial to creating and maintaining a sense of security in our relationships. You can transform a relationship by offering loving affirmations. It's worth the discomfort to tell someone the things you may wish you'd told them if you ever lost them.

Finally, it's important to recognise that intimacy may not just be expressed in the words you use. It may be in the hug that you're not accustomed to giving, or spending time together without a television on. Or buying someone a spontaneous gift to show you care. These things may initially feel a bit awkward if that's not how it's been done before, but now that you're becoming more intentional with your connections, you're in a position to rewrite the rules.

Ask yourself:

* Do your loved ones know how you feel about them?
* If someone has hurt you, what's your likely reaction?
* What makes you feel uncomfortable in your interactions?

 **PRACTICE**

Right now, reach out. Write a letter, a message or make a call and let a loved one know what you love about them. If you feel uncomfortable with the intimacy, acknowledge that. And then say or send it anyway.

Don't get hung up on their response, or lack of response. They may not yet be at a point where they are comfortable enough to give you the same affirmation back, or even graciously offer a proper thankyou. If you're switching up how things have always been done, it could come as a surprise to someone else, or even initially feel confronting. This step is more about you starting to offer love to others, not about anyone else giving that back to you. It can take time to create a new normal in a relationship.

Meaningful happens in a MOMENT. A *split-second* of HUMAN to HUMAN *interaction* *

Respond to bids for connection

The most important moments in our relationships are rarely grandiose or dramatic, making them easy to miss. Our interactions are made up of tiny choices and cues, and seemingly insignificant incidents. It's the collection of these moments that create the shape of our relationships. It's important to recognise that the people in our lives are constantly seeking connection with us. However, quite often, we're missing the cues.

Psychological researcher John Gottman teaches that a profound contributing factor to whether or not a relationship will flourish and last is how we respond to what he calls 'bids', which is a request to connect. According to Gottman, when this happens, we will respond by either turning towards the bid, turning away from the bid or turning against the bid. A bid can be as simple as your partner exclaiming, 'Look at that beautiful sunset!' Or it may be a friend telling you a story about something that happened in their workplace. It could be your child reaching up with a piece of toast to share it with you. Bids can be subtle or overt, verbal or found in body language.

When these bids occur, we have a choice. If your partner says, 'Look at that beautiful sunset!' you could say:

* 'Hmph' and not even look up. This is what Gottman would call turning away. You haven't acknowledged what they've said, either because you missed the bid, or you didn't bother responding.

* 'It's nothing special' or 'Can't you see I'm doing something?' which would be turning against a bid. You've squashed your partner and attacked their attempt to connect.

* 'Wow! You're right, it's gorgeous!' Here, you're turning towards their bid and affirming them.

Responding to bids doesn't generally require much energy or time from us. It's simply an acknowledgement of a statement, a response to a touch, or using body language that turns towards someone who is reaching out. One of the most important things is simply knowing that they exist and require a response. We've all witnessed people turning away from bids they could easily have responded to, without even realising they're doing it.

It's helpful to remember that a bid is more than what the actual words or gesture is about. It's a *call for connection*. By shutting someone down, you shut down the possibility for a moment of intimacy. It's important that we become conscious of the ways in which we can make consistent deposits of love into our connections.

Create shared narratives

Another way to establish a more meaningful connection with someone is through sharing a vivid experience with them. Think about a time when you went on an adventure with someone. Perhaps you travelled to another country, went to a music festival or ventured out on a camping trip. Getting out of the everyday grind and mixing it up is one of the fastest ways to create meaning in our relationships. When we keep meeting up in the same place, we tend to have the same types of exchanges. Move out of your standard environment and you'll shift away from your standard conversations. Even better, learn a new skill or throw in a challenge that you need to solve together and your bond will deepen in an instant. And the history of your relationship just became a lot more colourful.

Ask yourself:

* Do you have a tendency to do the same activities with the same friends?

PRACTICE

If you always go to the same café with the same person,
go for a bushwalk instead. Or sign up for a pottery class or drumming
class, dance lessons or a lecture series. Share something you love
or discover something new together. It's time to mix it up!

PRACTICE

Choose a person you'd like to connect with in a more meaningful
way and create a ritual with them. Use words, actions or objects to
create more depth, meaning and connection. Your ritual can be
as simple or as elaborate as you like.

Create rituals

Creating shared rituals helps us to create a feeling of closeness. Rituals are used by many cultures and traditions to instil depth, meaning and connection into an experience.

Rituals don't need to be elaborate or drawn-out. A couple could create a ritual whereby when they both get home, they could have a cup of tea together on the couch. This twenty-minute practice connects them, allows them to debrief about their day and gives them both insight into what the other is going through.

You create the ritual and you get to assign the meaning. The important thing is that it's something that brings you together in a moment of intimacy that may otherwise be missed if this gesture or activity wasn't there to punctuate the experience.

Ask yourself:
 * What are some of the rituals that you've already naturally integrated into your relationships?

Take time to upskill

Our relationships become more meaningful when we do a better job of them. We all feel our best when our relationships are firing, but this is rarely reflected in the time, energy and investment we put into our connections. The scales don't balance. In order to have extraordinary relationships, it's essential to recognise that showing up in them and loving well is a skill to be learnt.

Think about a time when you learnt something new. Perhaps it was a musical instrument, maybe it was a language. It's widely accepted these undertakings need time, energy, investment, commitment and practice. We'll often go to a teacher or read books, listen to podcasts or watch instructional videos. We are likely to pour hours and hours into becoming the best we can be at that particular skillset. Imagine if we invested that same amount of energy into learning how to be an amazing partner, an incredible father, a wonderful daughter, brother, friend or colleague. Inevitably, our relationships would be transformed.

What's your input into your relationships? This is directly reflected in the output. What you put in is what you get out.

Create connection with strangers

Never underestimate the impact you can have on someone you don't know. Even the smallest positive interaction can give their day a boost and create meaning where it wouldn't have otherwise been found.

Most of us are rushing through life, so completely preoccupied that we fail to acknowledge the people we pass throughout the day. In our next chapter, we'll learn about the science behind the energy of our interactions, but for now, imagine that you are a force field of loving kindness as you move through the world. This idea no longer just belongs in the realm of hippies or eastern healing modalities: it's for all of us.

Ask yourself:
* Do you avoid eye contact with people you don't know?

Be the change you want to see

It's a cliché but perhaps it's time to take it upon yourself to be the change you want to see in your relationships. Just like countries and cities, relationships have a culture – a certain resonance or energy in the dynamic – which can seem to be just 'the way things are'. Maybe you've got that friend who you always gossip with, or your family isn't very forthcoming. Maybe school pick-up is always a bit mundane. Just because it is doesn't mean it has to be. It only takes one person – in the couple or the family, the workplace or the friendship group – to shift the pattern towards a new way of operating. And there's no better time to start than now.

 **PRACTICE**

Do the practices in this book. Really commit to them.
It's easy to skip on through, but knowledge plus action is
where the true change will occur. And after you're done reading it,
go buy your next book on relationships or reserve a space
at a workshop. Get yourself ready to learn more.

 **PRACTICE**

Strike-up a conversation with a stranger. Perhaps it's
your Uber driver or someone walking their dog in the park.
Even a one-minute interaction with someone you don't
know can make their day as well as yours.

Chapter Five

Conversations

that

MATTER

Going below the surface

In the last chapter, we looked at ways to create more meaning in our relationships. Consider these the broad and necessary brushstrokes of a picture, as though we've just painted the background. It's now time to fill in the details.

You're catching up with a friend or you're in a taxi. You're at your mum's house or you're out for lunch with a colleague. You're having a real-life human encounter. The following suggestions are simple tweaks that will completely change the shape of the interaction. Fulfilling conversations *can* be generated, you just need to know how. Don't settle for another run-of-the-mill surface exchange; create one that feels like your souls just got that little bit closer.

Recipe for quality conversations

Be present. When you're with someone, *be with them*. Presence is a state of being. When you're present, you're not thinking about the future or the past; your focus is on what is happening in the very moment. Unfortunately, this kind of connection is pretty uncommon in an age when there is a tendency to be constantly multi-tasking. We're often thinking of the next thing before we've even finished the last. Add to this the prevalence of digital addiction and you'll find that we're rarely 'with' the people we're with.

Think about a time when you had a conversation with a person and they were *right there with you*. They looked into your eyes, hearing every word you said. Time stood still and there was an invisible energy flowing between you. They asked questions and seemed genuinely interested in the answers. These kinds of interactions feel good, don't they?

Work on remaining present for your people even when you have a billion other things running through your brain. Turn the TV off, take your phone off the table – in fact, leave it at the front door. There's no point making real-life contact if you're not truly showing up for it.

The degree of your presence will determine how much another person can open up to you.

You can sense when someone's not really listening, and others can tell the same when you're not with them in the present. You're only a little bit present? They can only offer a little bit of themselves. You wouldn't feel inclined to bare your deepest secrets to someone who is scrolling on their phone or checking the time, would you?

When you're present for others, they feel valued. When people feel valued, they feel safe to invest more of themselves. The more someone is invested in something – anything – the quality of it increases. One of the most impactful steps we can take towards something more meaningful in our relationships is to be more present with our loved ones.

TIP

* When you're talking to a loved one, consider it to be the most important moment of your day. Give them a level of presence as though you are the only two people on the planet.

* Turn your phone on aeroplane mode and put it in your bag.

* Don't answer your phone when you are in the company of others, especially at mealtimes or during important conversations.

Avoid small talk. There's nothing wrong with catching up on each other's latest washing machine purchase, but if that's all you're talking about, your connections can feel a bit one-dimensional. Small talk is something we can do on autopilot – it doesn't take much thinking or emotional engagement. It can glide across the surface of an interaction without even touching the sides. We leave feeling none the better for having had it, and sometimes worse. If you find you are caught in surface talk, it's time to delve a little deeper. We're about to find out how.

Avoid gossip. It's tempting to gossip. It's something we do to feel close to someone, especially when we don't know what else to say. Gossip creates a false sense of intimacy which, in the moment, might seem animated but later feels like junk food. Not only will gossip keep our interactions shallow, it also has a tendency to backfire and have insidious repercussions on relationships. How much can you trust someone who talks about others? How can you be seen as trustworthy if you do it? Plus, you know it's likely that you'll be next on their agenda, so there's only so much of your true self you'll expose to people like this.

Ask important questions. Asking questions, any questions, is imperative for someone to feel valued in an interaction. It shows that you're interested in them and invested in the moment. If you want to take it a little further, ask questions that matter more.

* First, ask someone about their passions and interests, and you'll see how soon they light up. It's amazing how brightly someone shines when asked a question that they genuinely enjoy answering. Give them the platform to talk about what they love.

* Then ask feeling questions. These kinds of questions help us to discover someone's underlying emotional motivators. *This* is where the real juice is.

I was speaking to a colleague who was telling me about her bathroom renovation. She was so excited about it, so I asked her what the best thing was about having a new bathroom. She shared that she was nursing her nervous system back to health after a very physically and mentally taxing time and having a proper bath each night made all the difference. All of a sudden, we were no longer talking about tiles.

What we are searching for in our interactions is not the what but the *why*. If someone is celebrating a new job, ask what part of it makes them most excited. If you see someone at a music festival, instead of asking them which bands they've seen, ask them what the highlight of their day has been – their what is far less interesting than their why. This potentially opens up a whole new conversation.

TIP

Some questions that draw meaningful answers:

* What has been your highlight?
* What has been the biggest challenge?
* What are you most grateful for?

# PRACTICE

Next time you're catching up with a group of friends or you're at a family event, suggest taking turns to reflect on what you're recently grateful for. It will open up the conversation to reveal things you perhaps weren't aware of. This simple practice works particularly well at significant events or when you haven't seen people in a while. There's an inevitable bonding that occurs and afterwards, everyone feels a little bit closer.

Listen to the answers. When someone is talking, most of the time, we are thinking. We're trying to filter the information they're giving us with the question, 'And how does this affect me?' and we're preparing a response. When we're only half there in conversations, we're missing so many clues and opportunities. When someone is talking, make it your mission to truly hear what they are saying. You will soon see that, behind the words, they are revealing greater truths, telling you about the way they best receive love, their fears, their passions, their needs. And now you're understanding them on a whole new plane.

Be familiar. Cut through all the preliminaries, and act as though you've known each other for years. My younger sister does this so well; she has this delightful way of behaving like she's everyone's best friend. She'll lean in while talking, she'll touch people on the arm, and be humorous, cheeky and warm. She feels like family to strangers and people love her for it.

A technique to help you create that familiar feeling and break down barriers is to ask for or offer a favour. I've met some of my best friends this way. If I see a mum on the beach on a sunny day looking desperate to get in the water, I'll offer to watch her children at the water's edge while she jumps in the ocean, and then ask her to return the favour. Pretty soon, our kids are playing together, we're doing a coffee run and we're planning a playdate.

Make each other laugh. Meaningful doesn't always have to be heavy. Making each other laugh will bond you just as quickly as revealing your deepest secrets. Seek opportunities to take yourself less seriously and get your banter on.

Make them feel good about themselves. Laugh at their jokes, be enthusiastic about their endeavours, tell them they look amazing, admire how clever they are. It costs you nothing to be friendly, frothy and kind. This doesn't mean you have to be fake, but rather to actively seek opportunities to affirm the people you interact with. When we do so, catching up is filling up.

Listen for important cues and follow them up. Listen out for what's been going on and what's coming up for the person you're talking to. They have a meeting coming up at work that they're feeling nervous about? They're applying to get into a course? They've been through a breakup and have a painful anniversary looming?

Take note and then follow up. Remember to be in contact on that significant day, whether it's a phone call or a message or you make a date to see them. Be ready to be there for them and to show that you care. This doesn't have to just be for the tough stuff, either. Show them that you're happy for their highlights and their celebratory moments as well.

TIP

* Don't rely on the fact that you will 'just remember' an important event or day. Put a reminder in your phone for the time and date so you're prompted to check-in.

Be caring, loving and energetically generous. Our body language speaks volumes more than our words. So it makes a huge difference to the quality of your interaction when you turn towards the other person, open your arms, make eye contact and smile encouragingly.

Something less known and discussed is what is happening on an energetic level when people interact. The Heart Math Institute is an organisation that uses scientific measures to map the energy exchange that occurs in human interactions. Their research has found that there is a reciprocation of electromagnetic energy produced by the heart when people touch or are interacting with each other. Our resonance is being biologically felt. This is amplified if even just one person in an interaction consciously adopts a sincere and caring attitude. When we shift into a more loving state there will be a measurable increase of coherence in the energy field. WOW.

More simply put, when we interact, we are sending invisible but very real energetic messages to each other. And when we intentionally care about each other, our hearts become more coherent. With this incredible knowledge, we can now recognise that those full-to-the-brim, heart-warming exchanges don't have to be a one-off. With the right intention and a generous attitude, we can consciously bring a feeling of depth and fulfillment to any exchange or interaction.

As humans, we thrive on meaningful connections, but our culture and our lives aren't always conducive to creating them. Digging deeper and becoming a more conscientious conversation partner can dramatically improve your relationships and interactions, whether it's with a close friend or a stranger on a plane. We can all use these tools to elevate our lives and connections, and perhaps brighten someone else's day as well. It might sound daunting but dig deep and be brave!

Chapter Six

HEALTHY
Boundaries

Identifying them and laying them down

Have you ever been in the position where you've wanted to say no but said yes? Or you made an offer you didn't truly want to follow through on? Maybe you've caught up with someone and walked away feeling deflated or exhausted, or you're the go-to when a demanding friend needs a problem fixed – again.

You're not alone. Most of us are moving through life following through on obligations, spending time with people who don't fill us up, letting ourselves be treated in a way that doesn't align with our needs, desires or inner truth. What kind of life is that? It's not deeply satisfying, and it certainly isn't meaningful. So let's talk about boundaries and how setting and sustaining them is a skill, one that most of us were never taught.

Boundaries are essential to healthy relationships and, ultimately, a healthy life. They're limits or guidelines you put in place to give others clarity about how to interact with you. Boundaries ultimately enable you to set the standard for how you'd like to be treated.

Sounds a bit formal, doesn't it? At first, you might feel weird trying to explain or set your boundaries with your loved ones. If you're a people-pleaser or in co-dependent relationships, it can feel excruciating to draw a line in the sand, for fear of offending someone or feeling the discomfort that can come with direct communication. However, it is worth persisting through the awkwardness as boundaries are vital to our wellbeing, and very closely linked with self-love.

Having boundaries is actually a gift to your loved ones. After all, what happens when you just go along with other people's requests? When we say yes but deep down we really feel no, it goes against our own inner truth. This self-betrayal creates an underlying feeling of resentment in us, that then grows. When resentment builds, it doesn't just magically disappear and, at some point, it will manifest.

Eventually, you'll blow up, walk away or blame the other person. We need to take responsibility and stop giving away our power. Rather than pointing the finger and blaming the other, we can recognise that if we say yes, we can't blame them for assuming we mean yes.

If you're changing things up, expect some ruffled feathers. When you begin practising new boundaries in existing relationships, it's possible – and actually very likely – that people will be offended or hurt, take things personally, misunderstand you or have emotional reactions, some of which may be quite big. Don't let this deter you. It's important to remember that healthy relationships aren't always comfortable, just like creating a healthy body isn't always comfortable. There's going to be a period of time when you're growing but eventually, you'll build your strength and it gets easier and feels more natural and integrated. Once you've built up your boundary muscles, you'll wonder how you ever managed life and relationships without them. Then you get to flex them.

Understanding your inner Yes and No

Before doing something, no matter how small, ask yourself, 'Why am I doing this?' If the answer is to get something in return, to feel approval, to be liked, to prove myself, to fit in, because I'm worried they'll leave, I'll feel guilty if I don't, because I really should ... it's a no.

If the answer is because it feels right, it lights me up, it comes from a place of love, it brings me joy, it nurtures me, it feels aligned, it's a yes.

Sometimes, your inner truth is loud and clear, shouting a big 'HELL YES!' or a 'F%#K NO!!' Most often, it's more subtle than that, and if we've never brought attention to it, it's likely that we are betraying ourselves over and over without even realising it.

Areas worthy of boundaries

* Your time.
* Your energy.
* Topics of conversation.
* Work obligations.
* How you wish to be communicated with.
* Technology (i.e. no phones during mealtimes).
* The time that you can give extended family members or friends who aren't aligned with your values.
* Housework.
* Eco-friendly living.
* How people interact with your children.
* Methods for dealing with conflict.

TIP

* **Your body is smart. It knows you better than your brain. So when you tell someone yes or no, pause, feel it out. Is there a feeling of contraction or tension in you? That's likely your inner truth communicating via your body to say no, this is not something you want to do. If there is a feeling of expansion, assurance, a breath out, it's a yes. Listen to your body. It's always sending you these useful self-love messages.**

NOTE: Sometimes you won't realise you've crossed your own boundary until you already have. Don't beat yourself up about it (remember, you're a self-lover now). Instead, take it as a signpost that you know now where to lay down your boundary line for next time.

 # PRACTICE

Make a list of the areas in your life in which you feel like you are over-compromising or being taken for granted. You'll know them – they are the moments, interactions, events and relationships that make you feel a little uneasy, unclean, unsure. Maybe you catch up with old friends who no longer align with you, or there's something you keep doing out of obligation that simply doesn't feel right. The first step is to acknowledge it.

 # PRACTICE

Look at the list you made, where you identified the areas you need to create boundaries. What's a one-liner you can use this week to help you say no, kindly and firmly, without excuses, lies or guilt? Practice saying it a couple of times so you're ready to whip it out when needed. Then commit to laying it down.

Small truth, bigger truth

Let's look at a boundary grey area. There are some things in life you don't want to do, but that doesn't automatically mean it's a no. For example, if it's my son's bedtime and he wants me to read him a story, I may ask myself if it's something I really want to do, and the answer may be no. I might be tired and ready to wind down for the day and wanting go to bed myself. But there are bigger truths involved. I want my son to sleep well, which is more likely if I've tucked him in and read him a story. I want him to feel safe, cared for and loved. Another bigger truth is that reading books engages his imagination. The biggest truth is that I'm a mother – I signed up for that role and this is part of it. So, in my moment of resistance, I access these bigger truths, desires and obligations, considering the bigger picture and long-term gain. In drawing on and acknowledging this, a no becomes a yes.

Boundary born-agains

An interesting thing can happen when you first start implementing boundaries. It can feel so good to finally be sticking up for yourself that you get a bit gung-ho. You're empowered, you feel ten-feet tall and you start laying down boundaries like it's nobody's business. Your delivery may even be a bit, well, brutal. People who find themselves doing this are Boundary Born-Agains. They're in the honeymoon phase of boundaries, so they can get a bit over the top, self-indulgent and forget about the bigger truths. As you build your boundary muscles, you'll learn it's a bit like a dance. The more you do it, the more you learn to navigate your small truth versus the bigger truth. You find ways to be as kind as possible, while still honouring your own needs.

Don't let boundaries be bad

Remember, the ultimate aim of the game is love. You need to stick to your non-negotiables, but having boundaries isn't an excuse to manipulate or control another person. You want to be implementing your boundaries alongside your fundamental building blocks, so don't forget your love, kindness and respect. Let me paint a picture here. Perhaps you don't like your partner's friend. They irritate the hell out of you. But your partner loves their friend and values the friendship. Making it a boundary that your partner never sees this person is controlling. If you use boundaries to manipulate others, it will come back to kick you in the ass. Boundary karma is real. So, instead, choose to limit the amount of time that *you* spend with that person, but be supportive and hands-off when your partner sees them or speaks to them, or even mentions them to you.

Let's do this – implementing boundaries

Most of us weren't taught or modelled boundaries, so creating them will take some practice. But don't worry, I've got you. Let's get started on learning how to properly set our boundaries. But just before we do, repeat after me: Boundaries are my right. I can set them and keep them, regardless of another's reaction.

Don't apologise when you lay down your boundary. 'I'm sorry, I'd love to, but I can't' is not a boundary. It's an excuse. No is healthy. No is normal. Saying No is not doing something wrong. Save 'sorry' for your genuine stuff-ups. If you apologise while laying down a boundary, you're undermining yourself.

Don't over-explain. No need to make excuses for your boundary. It's no one's business but yours. Simple.

Don't lie. The point of boundaries is living more authentically and having truer, more meaningful connections. Lying isn't a boundary; it's just a lie. And all that will do is sabotage the real connection you're searching for.

Don't palm it off if you don't mean it. 'I'm sorry, I have to head off but let's catch up for a coffee sometime.'

It feels like it softens the blow, and it might get you out of some mindless small talk, but check yourself before making offers or promises you don't want to keep. Otherwise, the other person may take you up on it, and you'll either have to follow through or make yet more excuses or promises.

Deliver with love. The idea of boundaries isn't to push your loved ones away or make people feel annoying, wrong or unloved. The intention is to create more meaningful, authentic connections, so deliver your boundaries with love and empathy. Sometimes you'll need to be firm, but you never need to be mean. You're stating your truth, not being an asshole. If someone has anxious tendencies or a fear of abandonment, your boundaries may feel threatening. Or if they had hopes and expectations of how something would be, it can be painful for them to realise that won't be the case.

Ideas on how to add a little extra love when creating a boundary:

* Seek alternative ways to support them that don't cross your boundaries. 'I'm needing some alone time to unwind from a big day. Can we connect tomorrow?'

* Acknowledge the painful reality of how our boundaries might impact our loved ones. 'I understand that it's challenging for you that I need to limit the amount of time I spend with your family.'

Draw the line with these one-liners

Can't come up with anything on the spot? Keep these handy one-liners close:

* 'I'm not going to be able to make it but thank you so much for thinking of me.'

* 'I'd love to be there for you but I'm in the middle of something. Can I call you later this afternoon?'

* 'I can see you're upset but please don't speak to me in that tone.'

* 'If you continue to speak to me like this, I'm going to need to take some space.'

* 'I'm going to take some space. I'll be back in twenty minutes to talk this through.'

* 'I won't be able to make it. I've realised I need to slow down, so I'm committing to less these days.'

* 'I love you and I want to support you, but I'm not willing to discuss this topic further.'

* 'I'd love to come over but I'll only be able to stay for an hour.'

TIP

✳ Don't answer phone calls from people you're struggling to hold boundaries with. Wait to get a message to find out what they want, or text them with something like 'I can't talk right now, what's up?' This buys you time to feel into what you really want before making agreements you might later wish you hadn't.

NOTE: Do this for others too. When I have a request to ask of a friend or family member, I'll text it to them or send a voice message, rather than calling. This gives them time and space to reflect on whether it's something they feel comfortable or able to help me with.

When boundaries receive difficult reactions

It's lovely to think the people in your life will celebrate your new boundaries. Perhaps even respect you for living your truth. Unfortunately, not everyone will.

Most humans are terrified of change. By bringing in new boundaries, you're doing things differently. You're adjusting the dynamic of the relationship, and they're relearning where they stand. And, honestly, they may have been benefiting from your previous lack of boundaries and might not be ready to let go of those perks.

Remember that other people's responses to your boundaries are not your responsibility. Your job is to learn how to handle *your* reaction to their response. It will be easy to feel angry, resentful, scared, hurt, regretful or guilty. That's going to be the test. You have every right to place limits on how you spend your time and energy. Put your hand on your heart and be sure to remind yourself of this in the moment.

Friendships and relationships with HEALTHY BOUNDARIES are the *happiest* because everyone gets to LIVE as their *truest selves*

You abandon and abuse yourself every time you say 'YES' when you want to say 'NO'. You call it loyalty/love/ friendship. Really, you're just hoping someone will see how amazing you are and choose you. It *doesn't work* that way. Choose yourself. That's how you teach them, **BY CHOOSING YOU**

Jennifer Arnise

Meeting – and celebrating – boundaries

The ability to welcome a boundary is a sign of emotional maturity. Although I might be initially disappointed when someone close to me sets a boundary, I also give them a massive high five. I'll say (sometimes in my head, and sometimes out loud) 'Go you! You're taking care of yourself!' I know resentment will be an unlikely thing in our relationship, because they're taking care of their own needs. Mostly, when a loved one with clear boundaries says yes, they really mean it. And that makes me feel pretty damn great.

A study was performed by Mississippi State University design student Peter Summerlin to research the impact of design on child development. Summerlin created a study to test how a group of children might feel and behave within a literal boundary – a fence.

The children were initially taken to a local playground that had no fence around the perimeter. They were encouraged to play as normal. They were then taken to another playground that had a clear fence around it. At the first playground, the children huddled around their teacher, feeling unsure of themselves and wanting to remain within her field of vision. At the second playground, they explored the boundaries and played freely and happily. The study concluded that when given limitations, children feel safer and more at ease to explore.

This is true also of boundaries within our adult relationships. They create clear parameters that offer us the safety of relating with more confidence and authenticity.

Bypassing boundary gridlock

So, what happens when two people in a relationship have opposing boundaries? How do you take another's needs into account while expressing yours?

Here are some suggestions:

* Identify which areas are non-negotiable boundaries and which are a preference. Compromise where you can on your preferences. Being generous lets the other person know you care and you're not being stubborn or a stickler just for the sake of it.

* Do your best to see their perspective and let them know that you understand how they feel.

* If you're on the receiving end of someone laying down a boundary that feels like it's opposed to your own, negotiate a solution that could work for you both. "I completely understand that spending regular time with my family makes you feel uncomfortable. It's really important to me that you're willing to come to some family events. Would you be open to going for one hour?'

* Remember that the aim here isn't to win. If the other person compromises on their boundary but resents you for it, it's not a win. It's the beginning of relationship difficulties or even a relationship breakdown.

* Create a boundary timeline. Perhaps neither of you can budge right now, but if it's not an urgent issue, consider coming back to revisit it at a later time to see if anything's changed. For example, perhaps you want to move homes, but your partner doesn't. You may choose to set a date to revisit the issue in three months to see where you are both at. People change, and so can boundaries.

* If it's a complete stalemate but you're not ready to let go of the relationship, seek help from a neutral person, like a therapist. A professional can help you navigate the issue and investigate a possible solution.

There can be times in a relationship when one person is doing a great job of laying down their boundaries, but it comes at a serious cost to the other. In order for a connection to last, it's important to take the other person into account.

Book in a boundary check-up

The word boundary can give a false impression of something that is fixed solid. But boundaries are – and need to be – malleable. As humans, we are ever-evolving, and our needs and perspectives are too. There are some boundaries you may never change, and you wouldn't want to. For example one of your boundaries might be that you will never be in an abusive relationship. But some boundaries are best created for a time, then lifted as your needs change, or a wound heals.

It's important to ask yourself if what you have created is a boundary or a barrier. For those with avoidant tendencies, boundaries can become a way to shut people out or avoid deepening in love. Although boundaries are important, so is the practice of leaning into intimacy and working through difficult emotions.

So, be careful not to hold on to boundaries for the sake of it, or you may not realise when they are no longer serving you or your relationships. Be sure to book in a boundary check-up and assess where you might like to lift your limitations. It's also a damn good chance to celebrate how far you've come.

Practice makes perfect boundaries

Setting boundaries is a skill you need on your relationship journey. It's going to take practice, but where you're headed is brighter and better than where you're at now. We've gone through the tools you'll need and the steps you'll take. Now you just need to practice it whenever necessary. The more you practice boundary setting, the easier it will become to tune into your truth. Over time, your boundaries will integrate with your inner voice, creating a way of life that aligns with your needs, desires and who you really are. You'll stop betraying yourself to receive love, which will encourage the people in your life to do the same.

I wish I'd had the COURAGE to live a life TRUE to myself, not the life OTHERS expected of me

Bronnie Ware

Chapter Seven

RELATIONSHIP
Dynamics

How conscious differences create harmony

There's an idea that sameness in a relationship creates compatibilty. Perhaps you look at a couple with similar attributes and assume that means they must be sailing along smoothly. But while it's important to have aligned core values and a deep friendship as the foundation of our relationships, sometimes the most harmonious connections come from stepping into opposite roles. Being on the same page doesn't necessarily mean being in the same state.

Even though we often think of opposites as being in opposition with each other, if we zoom out and look at the bigger picture, we can see how beneficial they can be for our relationships. Imagine night without day, or all day with no night.

Here are four relationship dynamics that may look opposing, but when seen in their wholeness, we have a new understanding of how they fit perfectly together. At times, these opposing roles may be taken on automatically, when we intuitively know what a situation is calling for. Other times, it has to be a conscious decision to understand where another person is at, what their needs are and offer them the opposite of what they are currently experiencing.

Understanding these roles is imperative to the survival of our relationships. This polarity can completely transform the way we relate, bringing more attraction and spark to intimate relationships, and reducing conflict to allow us to be seen and heard. Understanding and enacting these dualities is one of the greatest gifts we can give our loved ones.

Dynamic One: Presence and Surrender

In this dynamic, one person offers Presence to allow the other to Surrender. As we discussed back in Chapter Four, presence is one of the most important aspects of meaningful relationships. This is where you get to put it into practice. Presence is a state of heightened awareness that puts your entire focus on the current moment. In this case, that's the person in front of you. You're not thinking about something in the background and you're not mentally somewhere else. You are right there with them, rock solid, holding this state for an extended period of time.

This creates security for the other person, allowing them to surrender, open up and become vulnerable. Essentially, the person in the role of Presence is offering safety. They're giving the message, 'I'm here, I'm with you, I'm not going to leave, I've got you'. When someone feels held in this way, they are able to soften. In their role of Surrender, they are also offering a gift, and an opening. The message they're sending says, 'I'm unfolding, I'm dropping my barriers, I'm letting down my guard. I'm allowing you to see the real me'. Which feels pretty amazing for the person in Presence to witness and to receive.

This dynamic often appears during sexual encounters. When someone is in complete presence to another person, giving them their full focus, it creates safety for the other to unfold, blossom and experience full sexual expression. The best sex is often built on this foundation. Maybe you can think of a time when sex felt electric, connected and like you experienced an intense feeling of oneness. That's the yin–yang balance in physical form.

This dynamic also works well when someone is entering a new relationship after having been hurt in previous relationships. When the new partner can offer presence and patience, the uncertain person is more likely to feel safe to open to loving again.

The Presence and Surrender dynamic is also necessary for any kind of meaningful conversation. Think about how you feel when you're talking to someone and you know they're not really there with you. They're picking up their phone or glancing out the window. It doesn't motivate you to open yourself up and show true feelings, does it? Now think of those times when someone is in the zone with you. You're sharing something you haven't shared before and they are completely there, listening, affirming and energetically encouraging you. That's a true connection. There's an invisible bonding occurring, and it feels good.

Sometimes, in the moment, there will be a switching back and forth of roles in this dynamic – like in sex, or in a conversation where it's give and take. And at other times, it will just be one person holding a present space for an extended period of time while the other is free to safely surrender and unfold more and more.

Questions

* Think of a time when you were in a conversation with someone, and it didn't seem like they were being present with you. How did it feel?

* Think of a time when you were in a conversation with someone and they were right there with you. How did this effect the quality of the experience?

* Think of a time when you were able to hold space for someone and be present for them. What did that do for them, and how did it feel for you?

 # PRACTICE

Sit down with a loved one and set a timer for three minutes.
Ask them to describe the greatest challenge they have experienced
in their life, including telling you about the circumstance and feelings
at the time. Remain in complete presence while the other person opens
up. You're not judging their words, you're not interrupting. You're
energetically with them. After three minutes, switch roles, reset
the timer and have them ask you the same question.

Afterwards, have a chat about any realisations you had about
your experience in the varying roles.

* How did it feel to offer complete presence?

* How did it feel to receive presence?

* What was it like to share?

* Did you feel that you were able to easily reveal yourself
or was this a challenge?

Dynamic Two: Direction and Flow

In this dynamic, the person in Direction is offering assurance, clarity and, you guessed it, direction. The message they are giving the other person is, 'I've got this. I can see clearly where we need to go, you can relax, leave it up to me'. The person in Flow can breathe easy. It takes the pressure off and allows them to receive. They, in turn, are offering trust. The message they're giving is, 'Lead the way, I trust that you've got this, take me with you'.

This dynamic often appears in the decision-making process. The decision could be as small as where to go for dinner or as monumental as the possibility of moving to a new country. If somebody is burnt-out, indecisive or feeling confused, it can be such a gift to have someone else take the reins. From the other angle, if someone is inspired and has clarity and conviction, it can feel great to offer direction and have someone else jump on board with their vision.

Questions

* Which of these roles do you feel you have a tendency towards? Direction or Flow?

* How does it feel when you find yourself in the opposite role to your natural tendency?

NOTE: In healthy relationships, it's important we allow our loved ones to influence us. Yes, we may have boundaries, and yes, it's fine to be focused, but if your need to control is so strong that you consistently refuse to take on suggestions, new ideas or plans that are different from your own, you're heading towards dysfunction. Be open to being open.

 # PRACTICE

Organise a half- or full-day date with a friend or partner. One person takes the lead while the other is in flow. The person giving direction maps out the day with activities to do together. The other person simply goes along with it, not knowing what has been planned.

At the end of the date, have a chat about how you felt in your role.

* If you were in Flow, was it a welcome relief or was it difficult to let go of control?

* If you were in Direction, was it fun to lead, or was it nerve-wracking to make the decisions?

* Did you feel trusted by the other person?

Next time, switch roles for another date, so you can both experience the other side of this dynamic.

* If we want our relationships to be **MEANINGFUL**, we need to *override* this **BRAIN** logic with **HEART** logic

Dynamic Three: Support and Shine

In this dynamic, Shine shines bright. This type is often creative, ambitious and radiant. And Support is in no way threatened by Shine's light. In fact, Support gets a kick out of either being witness to this light or being the on-ground support. The message the support person is giving is, 'I see you in your beauty/creativity/glow, and I'm happy to step back from the spotlight and support you to be your best self' or 'I get real pleasure in witnessing you shine' or 'I love supporting this project as it comes into fruition'.

Shine has something to share with the world and it's shimmering, sometimes even bursting, from within. This may be a constant aspect of their personality. For example, they're naturally charismatic, always the life of the party; they walk into a room and light it right up. Or maybe they have a creative project they're birthing that's adding some magic to the world. The beauty of being around Shine is that it's a joy to be swept up in the radiance they are putting out into the world. They pull you into the magic of the moment and it's a captivating experience.

It's like the interplay of roles in Acroyoga, a physical practice that combines movement and poses from both yoga and acrobatics. Most of the time in Acroyoga, it's one person's role to be the base. The other is the flyer. The base is solid and supportive; they position their body so that it creates a strong foundation for the flyer. The flyer is usually balanced atop the base in a more precarious position, flying high in full glory and radiance, usually creating a graceful and beautiful position or form. Sometimes, there is a dual dynamic and the participants take turns and switch roles, and sometimes one person is always the base and the other is always the flyer. So too with Support and Shine. In some relationships, two people will trade off these roles, depending on whose turn it is to shine brightly. In other relationships, one person takes the Support position most of the time, allowing Shine to shine.

 # PRACTICE

Sit down with another person and set a timer for two minutes. Choose a topic about which you feel extremely passionate – something that lights you up and gets you really excited – and talk about it until the timer goes off. Alternatively, come up with a performance of sorts. A song, dance or poem.

While you take the stage, the other person supports you energetically by being completely present. Then switch and let the other person shine while you support. Discuss.

* Which of these roles did you feel more comfortable in?
* How did it feel to be playing the role you're not as comfortable taking?

 # PRACTICE

Next time you are in a situation in which someone has a lot to express – whether they are hurting, feeling unstable, or even having a wild orgasm – can you hold that space for them? Without judgement, and without taking their energy personally?

* What happens if you allow, even encourage, them to release and you let them know you have their back?

* What course does the expression take?

Questions

* Which of these roles do you feel you have a tendency towards? Support or Shine?
* How does it feel when you find yourself in the opposite role to your natural tendency?

Dynamic Four: Strength and Expression

In this dynamic, the person in Strength is holding space for the other in Expression. They are sending the message, 'I can hold this for you, I can allow you to express without judgement, I'm your rock, I am solid'. It's a similar dynamic to Presence and Surrender, but a much more amplified version. You may find that Presence and Surrender morphs into Strength and Expression. When someone drops their barriers and surrenders, sometimes they are moved to express something big.

Because the person in Expression is having a release, it can be quite intense. The person in Strength needs to step up, be able to hold the intensity of what's coming their way, and not take it personally. The person in Expression is communicating: I am hurting/confused/in pain/angry/feeling a lot and I need to let it out. Or perhaps: I am in trouble and need help.

This dynamic often appears in conflict, during difficult times or when something has happened, either within the relationship or outside of it, that needs to be resolved and processed. It can also happen when one person has hit a mental breaking point or physical crisis and needs support. An example is childbirth, where one or more people will step into the role of Strength in order to hold the birthing person's powerful Expression.

It's important to recognise that if someone needs to express themselves and you're holding space for that, it's no excuse for them to be abusive towards you. Remember the boundaries you laid out in Chapter Five. You can let someone know you are open to hearing their feelings and you may even let them storm it out a bit to release their charge. However, if at any point it feels like it's crossing your boundaries or is unsafe for you, you have the right to draw that line.

It's also important to note that while this dynamic does pop up, it's usually in heightened times or during a crisis. It's for a phase. If this is a regular mode of communication in your relationship/s, you may need to check if there is an addiction to drama at play. If this type of experience is happening constantly, it's worth checking in. Bringing awareness to drama addiction is imperative to begin to learn to spot the patterns and shift it.

Questions

* Which of these roles do you feel like you have a tendency towards? Strength or Expression?
* Think of a time when you needed to express or release and someone was your Strength? How did that feel?
* Think of a time when you were the Strength for someone else? How did that feel?

*There's a balance and harmony in COMBINING *differences*

The lighthouse and the ocean

With all four of these dynamics, it's useful to draw upon the analogy of a lighthouse and an ocean. A lighthouse stands strong, a solid presence that offers direction and support. The ocean moves around it, flowing and ever-changing. One moment it can be calm, the next it can be wild.

It's the duality of these dynamics that create a balance. Sameness can mean a lack of charge or too much charge. If two people are in Expression, there can be a gridlock. If no one is holding space or listening, things can blow up. If two people are in Flow, you may never leave the house ('You decide' 'No, YOU decide'). Two people in Presence makes for a great meditation, but not necessarily expansive sex.

So what happens if you're both feeling the same way? Often, it's a matter of learning to assess who needs priority in a certain role at that time. As we apply the work of conscious relationships, we learn to dance that dance. This is when our building blocks come into play. We've learnt about kindness, grace and support, and here is where we put them into practice.

It can also help to have a code. Agree on some sentences or words that will be your lifeline in the moment. They'll send a clear message to the other person about what you need, penetrating the situation and shifting the dynamic in a second.

Here are some examples:

* 'Can you be my sounding board? I need to get something off my chest.'

* 'I need you to be present right now. Can you do that for me?'

* 'I'm here for you, I'm not going anywhere.'

* 'Can you back me on this? I'm going to need support.'

* 'I need you to take direction on this one.'

* 'Can you please trust me with this?'

* 'I'm here for you, the whole way through this.'

* 'I'm on an edge. Can you please be my rock?'

* 'I've got you.'

You may not always be available to be what the other person wants or needs, and that's okay. It's important to protect your own energy. Explain that you'd love to help, and perhaps offer an alternative time or way you can be there for them.

As this duality appears in relationships, it also appears within us as individuals. We all have our inner yin and yang. We likely have a tendency to be more of one than the other – some of us are more like the lighthouse and some more like the ocean. Understanding the spectrum of these dynamics brings self-awareness to our behavioural tendencies. It can also shine a light on aspects that we can practice strengthening. When we develop these qualities within, we can access them more freely when a real-life scenario calls for them.

Understanding your own duality is a game-changer. Understanding duality within relationships can alter your connections exponentially. People say opposites attract, but really, opposites can take your sex life to new heights, help you find more harmony and joy in your day-to-day interactions and uncover calm and effective ways to deal with conflict. Now, *that's attractive*.

## Chapter Eight

MEET The Four MONSTERS

Why loving relationships break down

It would be remiss of us to explore how to have more meaning in our relationships without acknowledging some of the obstacles that prevent us from experiencing it. So let's take a look at the elephant in the room or, in this case, the monster.

Meet the Four Relationship Monsters. These are usually the underlying causes of what is creating disharmony in our relationships. Unfortunately, it is common that we deny their existence until it's too late. Identifying which monster is at play and knocking it on the head will result in less damage to our connections and will help prevent relationship breakdown.

Monster One: Resentment

Resentment is one of the biggest dangers to a relationship. It can creep up on us, slowly building, like a version of anger but more bitter and insidious. Anger will usually blow up and show itself, whereas resentment can bubble beneath the surface for a very long time. Eventually, it can be catastrophic.

When we feel resentment, we often don't want to acknowledge it. Or we try to and don't get the result we hope for. Resentment is often the result of something that feels unsolvable that you've been forced to accept but haven't truly accepted in your heart.

In order to deal with this, you first need to identify the cause of your resentment. Ask yourself, 'Why am I feeling like this?' and try to pinpoint exactly where it's coming from.

Then it's time to take action. This will vary, according to why you're feeling the resentment in the first place. For example, if you're feeling jealous and that's causing resentment, the action you might take could be asking yourself, 'What is it about my lifestyle that needs to shift so that I'm not feeling resentful?'

If you're feeling resentful because of the behaviour of a loved one, this will often need to be communicated in order for things to shift. Talking it through with the person you're feeling resentful towards can bring clarity and reconcile the issue. This obviously isn't always possible and may not play out the way you hope as people aren't always ready to own their actions. Then there will be times when a loved one *will* own their actions, and even make the changes needed to reconcile the issue, but resentment still lingers. If either of these scenarios occurs, talking to a counsellor can be helpful.

The important thing is to get to the bottom of it, whether that's on your own journey or sorting it out with the other person. If resentment doesn't shift, it grows. The more powerful it is, the greater its potential to be incredibly destructive. If you ever sense resentment taking hold, be sure to address it immediately so it doesn't escalate to danger.

Monster Two: De-transfiguration

In Chapter Three, we looked at the concept and practice of Transfiguration and the impacts of perceiving your relationships and loved one/s through a positive lens. This monster is the exact opposite. When we de-transfigure someone, we are charging up a negative perspective of the person and our relationship with them. We perceive all of this person's actions as unfavourable.

De-transfiguration most often occurs later in established relationships. New relationships usually involve hormones flying around that keep us feeling quite excited about the other person. Over time, this can change, especially in intimate, long-term partnerships. When you throw stress, lifestyle changes, responsibilities or kids into the mix, de-transfiguration can be quite common.

Just like resentment, this is a dangerous monster, often starting with small issues but then gaining momentum and growing fast. Let's look at how this can happen in just a few steps.

It might begin with a communication problem. One of those little fights that's really a simple misunderstanding. These unresolved misunderstandings can lead to further misunderstandings, and this is where we begin to assume the worst of each other. Negative perceptions lead to de-transfiguration. De-transfiguration becomes the lens through which we perceive all the other person's behaviours. Even innocent or positive acts are seen as negative. Finally, everything the other person does is witnessed through this lens. It appears to us that they are behaving selfishly, hurtfully and with ulterior motives. You now see them as a horrible person, and you probably let them know as much.

Pause. Few people will respond well to being told how bad they are. When people are criticised and made to feel small, they lose motivation, drop any effort and dig in their heels. So if you're constantly pointing out someone's flaws, you're not actually solving the problem; you're amplifying it. The other person is unlikely to feel motivated to be anything but your perception of them, behaving in a way that affirms your negative viewpoint. You'll see their lack of effort as even more reason to be angry, resentful, critical and hurt as your perception becomes your reality.

You can see the destructive loop this creates and how, eventually, there will be a point of no return. People are likely to become what they are repeatedly told they are. Perceiving your relationship in a negative light means you are likely to either end up experiencing disconnection or constant disharmony, or breaking up.

When it comes to this monster, we want to catch it before it creates too much havoc. Once you've engaged a negative mindset, it's *very* hard to shift it. De-transfiguration is fuel for the ego and it's difficult to deny ourselves of that. So, a huge kudos to anyone who can spot that they are de-transfiguring another person. Acknowledging that you are doing this with your partner, relative or colleague is a big step, and it's the first move we need to make if we want to break the cycle. Next, we need to be willing to take the necessary steps to turn it around. How do we do it? It will take effort. This is where we draw on the practice of Conscious Transfiguration, the choice to love, appreciate, uphold and affirm. When we consciously transfigure a person, we shift our focus back to what is working and wonderful about them.

This is not to say you should stay in a relationship that is abusive or unhealthy, and just positively 'think your way' into it all being okay. Instead, simply reassess your current relationships and ask yourself if you've got into a negative rut. Maybe you've become hypersensitive and you're taking things too personally. Perhaps you're missing something wonderful that's right in front of you. De-transfiguration can cause you to forget the beautiful memories and the best qualities the other person possesses.

Our brains naturally have a negativity bias. This is due to ancestral survival psychology in which paying attention to pessimistic possibilities and negative past experiences increased the likelihood of survival. So it's no wonder that we fall into patterns of noticing and focusing on the negative traits of our loved ones. The following Conscious Transfiguration exercises will help you acknowledge the good, thereby giving your relationship the credit it deserves, and redirecting your brain to recognise when you're having positive experiences in real-time.

 # PRACTICE

* Create a Transfiguration journal. Make a daily commitment to write down three positive qualities this person has. If it's someone you're close to, it can be powerful to also write down a positive or pleasant memory from your shared history.

* Reflect on how you met or a great chapter in your relationship.

* Remind yourself of the nice things this person does for you and/or the nice things they've done in the past.

* Speak positively about this person to other people. When I had my first baby, in many ways, my relationship fell apart. I was de-transfiguring my husband – he knew it, and so did I. My practice of Conscious Transfiguration was to talk to my baby (within my husband's earshot) and tell him what was wonderful about his dad. Additionally, when we went to marriage counselling, I opened up about my challenges but I also made sure to mention all the wonderful qualities my husband has. When we looked at the ratio, the good far outweighed the bad.

* Appreciate and affirm any of the things you want to see more of. Appreciation is a huge motivator for humans. If you affirm their good qualities, they are likely to display them more often. If you continue to show appreciation, these qualities are likely to amplify. It becomes a positive cycle.

* Remember that we are all human and no one is perfect. Take yourself back to the building block of Grace and ask yourself if you need to be extending some understanding.

✳ Notice the human things about another person. When we de-transfigure somebody, we have a tendency to demonise them. To consciously transfigure is to remind yourself that this is a human, and this human has a soul. Many cultures talk about the eyes being the window to the soul and there are different teachings that encourage us to look into someone's eyes and remind ourselves of that. Take time each day to look into each other's eyes and say, 'I love you'. This moment of intimacy helps to register and appreciate the humanity and beauty in one another.

✳ Practice an open-eye meditation together. This transfiguration practice involves sitting opposite another person and looking into their eyes. You can even hold hands if it feels right. To begin, close your eyes and take some deep breaths to bring yourself into a present state. When you're ready, open your eyes and look into the eyes of the person in front of you. It can help to focus on one eye, so perhaps you both focus on the left. Soften your gaze and relax. Hold the gaze for a few minutes, maybe longer. Remember to breathe and, yes, you can blink too, it's not a staring competition! The exercise may feel really intimate and that's ok. It will be different for everyone. For some, they will enter a meditative state where time seems to stand still. Others will start to see different colours, shapes or visions. Some will feel like they are seeing straight into the soul of the other person and experience a feeling of oneness, unity or heart-opening. For others, it can feel like energy is rushing through their bodies. Some people cry, while others dissolve into fits of giggles. One thing is for sure: it's impossible to stay angry or de-transfigure in the moment that it's happening.

Monster Three: Complacency

Our loved ones – especially family members or intimate partners – quite often don't get the best of us. The more familiar we are with people, the more likely we are to be rude, dismissive or complacent. We speak to them and treat them in a way that we would never speak to or treat our boss, an acquaintance, or someone we've just met. Yes, this is because we're familiar with them, but there's a difference between feeling comfortable and being complacent. Being comfortable means dropping your masks, being authentic and intimate. Being complacent means dropping the building blocks, and when this happens, the house starts to fall apart.

At the beginning of a relationship, complacency is rarely a problem. In the early stages of intense love, it's so easy to be enthusiastic about going the extra mile, making the effort and coming up with creative things that we can do for our partner. As time goes on and as hormones calm down, we often stop making these efforts and start taking loved ones for granted.

Imagine if you bought a house. It looks shiny and bright in the beginning, but if you just left it, with no regular gestures of maintenance, the paint would fade and the cracks would appear. It would suffer from inattention and begin to atrophy. The longer it was left, the more difficult it would be to recover.

You'll often hear people say that relationships are hard work, and it's true that all relationships have their difficult moments and challenging phases, but a lot of the difficulty that necessitates the hard work shows up when we've stopped investing and left things for too long. Relationship educator Alison Armstrong offers some insight into why we slip into complacency. 'Our brain is constantly trying to save energy – it's very aware of the cost of paying attention and looks for places it doesn't have to. For example, it decides that it already knows everything worth knowing about your partner, friend, family etc., and stops paying attention to the people most important to you.'

If we want our relationships to be meaningful, we need to override this brain logic with heart logic. We need to recognise that the closer we are to someone, the more important it is to invest in that relationship. After all, these are the relationships that will likely be there for longer.

When we lose a loved one, whether due to a move, a break-up or a death, we feel grief not just for the loss but for how we could have done things differently. What if we knew we had limited time with our loved ones? How would we act and be? Non-complacency is doing these things *now*. It seeks out opportunities to love more fully and generously. It's a commitment to progression, to the evolution of your relationship, to the building blocks. It's a fervour to tackle the difficulties, the things that normally get swept under the carpet or put in the too-hard basket.

When we're in a relationship and complacency has crept in, it's easy to think that your loved one is the problem. Maybe you think they're nagging or complaining, but perhaps the problem is that you're offering the best version of yourself to everyone but them. It could also be that you're avoiding dealing with the tough stuff, issues that you hope will just go away.

So, on a regular basis, invest in your relationship's 'house' – give it fresh coats to keep it bright and tender care to keep it not just maintained but thriving. What does this look like? You get to tailor that for your relationships. First, identify the people in your life who you would be most devastated to lose. Next, make a plan of what you would like to commit to. And then honour that like you would a work meeting. Perhaps it's a regular romantic date night with a partner or putting a reminder in your phone to call your mum every week. It could be carving out daily playtime with your children.

What you'll find is that the rest of your life will rearrange itself to fit in with your commitment to the greatest loves of your life.

Finally, it's important to realise that complacency can sometimes be a genuine result of simply getting stuck in a rut, being busy or assuming that the other person will always be there. This can and will cause issues in a relationship, but far more serious is the complacency that comes when someone is no longer invested, has tapped out or doesn't bother making an effort. The biggest danger is when someone doesn't see the relationship as something worth making an effort for. When this happens, complacency has morphed into indifference and the relationship will be on a serious downhill spiral unless you actively and consciously make the effort to turn things around.

Monster Four: Poor Communication

Many relationship breakdowns and conflicts stem not from a lack of love, but rather from not knowing *how* to communicate love with ease and flow. The love is there, or it certainly was to begin with, but it's been worn down over time as we keep missing the mark with each other. Poor communication leads to conflict, which leads to misunderstandings, which leads to distance and often breakdown.

It's important to recognise that communicating well is a skill, an important one, that most of us never learnt. As a result, we don't understand how to best relate and we often send the wrong message or misunderstand each other's motivations. Most of the time, there is a good reason for everything that another person does. However, we are quite often taking things the wrong way or delivering our own messages without awareness or sensitivity.

Like with anything, when we upskill in this area, it will come more naturally to us over time. We will learn to avoid the stumbles and the mishaps that can have serious effects on a relationship's chances of survival. It will also certainly help us to avoid expending the huge amount of energy required to deal with the mess that miscommunication can create.

It's important to understand that this monster has a large scope. On one end of the spectrum, poor communication is quite innocent – simply a lack of education or someone genuinely missing the mark and another person getting hurt. As things degenerate, however, we're heading towards the other end of the spectrum, where communication becomes the way in which we make another person feel small and shut them down.

Some of the ways Poor Communication can show up:
* Missing the mark or misreading a situation.
* Having different communication skills.
* Having different communication styles due to coming from different cultural or family backgrounds.
* Avoiding difficult or uncomfortable conversations.
* Taking things personally.
* Failing to check in or make contact.
* Avoiding confrontation.
* Confronting issues without care or tact.
* Making assumptions.
* Missing bids for connection.
* Failing to communicate a need to connect.
* Giving the silent treatment.
* Using closed body language.
* Being passive-aggressive.
* Interrupting.
* Being defensive.

Poor communication becomes particularly toxic when it is not the result of a lack of skill or tact, but rather a cruel attitude. When this is the case, we are heading into dangerous territory. Things can turn particularly nasty when we start to communicate with our loved ones in contemptuous or belligerent ways. Snarky one-liners, sarcastic comments, belittling, mocking or being insensitive to another person's triggers. Refusing to listen to the other person's point of view and invalidating their feelings. Being arrogant and critical in the delivery of your message. Using an intimidating tone. These are all not just poor communication, but a lack of respect, and respect, as you'll remember, is one of our fundamental building blocks and an integral aspect of any healthy relationship.

It's important that we mature in the way we communicate with our loved ones. We need to become conscious of the words that come out of our mouths, to craft our sentences lovingly and with care, and to seek connection with the things we say. It's a very small percentage of people that this comes naturally for. So one of the greatest ways you can counter poor communication is to educate yourself in ways to better get your message across. Two small yet profound books that may help smooth the way are *The Four Agreements* by Don Miguel and *The Five Love Languages* by Gary Chapman. Taking on-ground action by speaking to a therapist, attending a workshop, participating in an online course or listening to podcasts that will help you upskill in this area will also create rewarding results.

Over time, if left unchecked, each of the four monsters can cause the breakdown of a relationship. The best way to prevent this is to recognise the danger as early as possible, take action to knock it on the head, and then take continued precautions to ensure it doesn't come back. Do the exercise on the next page as many times as needed for every monster that rears its head in your life. Your relationships will be stronger, better and healthier for it.

# PRACTICE

* Identify a relationship in your life in which you think you may have a monster at play.

   * Which monster is it? Resentment? De-transfiguration? Complacency? Poor Communication? Remember, these monsters can also team up – there's every chance that you've got more than one monster causing damage to a single connection.

* Identify the specific nuance in how the monster expresses itself.

Resentment – where do you think the resentment stems from?
a) Jealousy
b) Feeling hurt by a past incident
c) Feeling hurt by ongoing behaviour
d) Feeling restricted
e) Other

De-transfiguration – what are some of the ways in which you de-transfigure this person?

Complacency – in what areas have you become particularly complacent?

Poor Communication – look back at the list of poor communication examples. What are some of the ways in which you communicate poorly in in this relationship ?

After you've identified your monster, ask yourself:
* What is one commitment I can make today to begin to counter this?

Chapter Nine

CONFLICT

AND

Challenge

How to handle the tough times

The important question isn't whether or not conflict will happen, but how you can best handle it when it does. Most of us have never learnt what to do when challenges appear, so what we end up doing is making it worse or escalating a situation that could have been nipped in the bud.

These are some of the methods we can use when things get tough. The intention here is to approach disagreements in a way that prevents relationship damage, and to understand ourselves and our loved ones that little bit better.

Attitude to conflict

The most important thing to recognise upfront is that one of the greatest influences on our experience of conflict is our attitude towards it. Most people have never been modelled healthy conflict and reconciliation methods. As a result, our conditioning tells us that conflict is negative, and for good reason – the majority of us have witnessed or experienced conflict as aggressive, passive-aggressive, nasty and damaging.

Healthy relationships call on us to reframe what it means to be in conflict and to then retrain ourselves to trust and understand that. Rather than seeing a disagreement as a disaster, we learn to recognise it as an opportunity.

As ambitious as this may sound, everything mapped out in this book so far is designed to be the very foundation on which we can create enough safety in our challenges to find the gold. Staying conscious in conflict is far more achievable with a culture of love, kindness, respect and grace, and with boundaries, presence and listening. As we build these qualities into the fabric of our connections, we slowly learn that we can override our conditioning because we, and the person we are in conflict with, have an established agreement that we've got each other. This helps us to remember not to take things personally or see conflict as a reflection of the quality of our relationship.

When conflict is established as a space for safe expression, our challenges can become one of our greatest gateways for relationship growth and the transcending of old patterns. We begin to understand ourselves and our loved ones on a whole new level, which carves a path for greater intimacy, more understanding and less conflict down the road.

Accept your differences

We're different humans, so we're going to have differences. We come into relationships with our stories, triggers, conditioning, personality traits and life goals. There will be some differences and points of contention that will *always* be there and, as a result, some issues that can never be fully resolved.

Now before we go on, let's acknowledge that our thoughts, mind and personalities are malleable. We can heal our past trauma, transcend our conditioning and learn new ways of being. When people declare, 'That's just who I am', it's not as definitive as it sounds. We can change – if we *want* to.

But (there's always a but) ...

We're not always ready to change. And there are plenty of things we shouldn't have to change. We're not all meant to be the same. We may have totally different ways of being and doing to our loved ones and that's okay. The sooner we understand and accept this, the better. There can be an expectation, particularly in intimate relationships or in parent–child dynamics, that the other should be like us; that sameness is equal to goodness.

The way to build a great relationship isn't to change your loved ones but to find the best systems to help you live with the differences. Rather than putting all our energy into trying to make someone like us or make ourselves like someone else, it's essential that we surrender to, and even celebrate, our diversity.

It's important to point out a subtlety here. There's a distinction between appeasing someone and accepting your differences. When you're appeasing someone, you're nervous or scared to be real around them or voice your true concerns. When you've accepted your differences in a relationship, you're gracefully acknowledging that multiple realities can exist. You haven't changed or suppressed who you are, you're simply choosing not to aggravate the differences.

Prevention is better than cure

We've already established that some conflict is inevitable but that doesn't mean that all conflicts are. There are plenty of conflicts that can be prevented. As you integrate the teachings in this book, you will be averting certain problems that might usually be issues of contention in your relationship/s just by doing the work. When you're arguing about the little things, there is usually an underlying cause. If you've created a nice solid foundation of building blocks, you're giving yourself the love you deserve, you understand each other's boundaries, you're having meaningful interactions and you're dealing with your Monsters, you'll find that you and your loved one/s have less to fight about.

Proceed with care

There's a high probability that if you go into a difficult discussion with guns blazing (or even just pointing the finger), the conversation is only going to go in one direction. The other person's nervous system will react to the perceived threat and once activated, it will be very hard for them to be rational and kind. Their body will tell them they need to protect themselves, so they'll either get their emotional boxing gloves on or they'll bail as quickly as possible. These reactions are likely to aggravate the situation further, and all of a sudden, the conflict will become about the reaction rather than the initial issue. Things get messy.

Unfortunately, most difficult conversations are approached in this way and most people respond defensively. It can take some patience to remember this when you're upset and want to get an issue off your chest, but once you start to take a more gentle approach and you see the positive results, you'll have far more motivation to begin those tricky discussions with awareness and care.

Centre yourself. Take some time to process your feelings before the conversation. Journalling, whether putting pen to paper or in an app, can often help you sort through your feelings. Processing your thoughts by speaking them out loud or into a voice recorder may help too. It can also be beneficial to speak to a therapist to help get you clear on what's going on for you and what you'd like to say.

Use 'I' statements. The golden rule that a lot of Therapists recommend for effective communication is to begin your statements with 'I' or 'I feel'. This makes whatever you say about you rather than the other person, so they will be less likely to automatically become defensive. This has you off to a better start than if you come out with accusatory statements that blame the other person for your feelings. Some additional advice from Gary Chapman, author of *The Five Love Languages*, is that we present our desires as requests rather than demands. Instead of telling someone what they've done wrong or what they should be doing – 'You never ... You always ... You should ... You shouldn't ...' – turn it into a request and it will be far better received. For example, instead of, 'You never make me feel important. You always prioritise your friends over me' try 'I love spending time with you. These days, I feel like we haven't been doing that as often. Would you be open to setting aside a date night each week?'

When your approach doesn't work

There will be times when, regardless of how conscious you are in your approach, language and intention, things still turn pear-shaped. If you see things going downhill, try to catch them! Cut through the building tension with a vulnerable reminder of your good intent, or an honest compliment of the other person's character. This offers them reassurance that you are not attacking them personally and calms their nervous system down enough to enable them to hear you.

You could say, 'I'm sorry, I don't want you to feel attacked or like you have to defend yourself. I'm only bringing this up with you because I love you, and I know it's better for our relationship that we talk about these things. I'm totally open to understanding your perspective.'

Be aware of triggers

A trigger is an emotional activation based on a past memory. Our personal histories are punctuated by incidents – both positive and negative – that leave a lasting imprint. When something happens in the present that reminds us (either consciously or subconsciously)

 # PRACTICE

* Has something been bothering you in one of your relationships?

* Have you been feeling put out or wishing things looked differently? Put pen to paper and write down your concern or hurt.

_____

_____

_____

_____

* Then, create a statement using the words 'I' or 'I feel' and pose it as a request, like in the example on the previous page. The next step is to make the call or meet up and try it out in real life!

_____

_____

_____

_____

of a past experience, we can be immediately catapulted into the emotion we once had, as though we are experiencing the original incident in real time. This is what we call a trigger.

It's important to understand the effect that triggers can have on our behaviour and interactions. Small triggers can create a slight shift in our mood and then we may carry on. Bigger triggers can have us completely overwhelmed with emotion. As a result, if we are triggered by something someone says or does, it can create a larger response than expected. If that person doesn't realise that they have triggered a childhood wound, for example, it can appear that we are overreacting, being overly sensitive or behaving out of character. That doesn't mean that what we're upset about isn't legitimate, but if it's creating an extremely strong reaction in us, this is often an indication that past issues have arisen and become involved, which will then prevent us from showing up with clarity in the present moment. We're basing our current reality on past circumstances.

The next time you feel triggered, it can help to take a moment to pause and ask yourself, 'What does this situation remind me of?' Is there a certain memory surfacing for you? And when someone blows up, gets mad or suddenly speaks to you in a way you don't expect, remember that there is every likelihood that this person is reacting because something deep has been triggered within them. It's not an excuse to allow people to treat you badly, nor are your triggers an invitation or allowance for you to treat others badly. However, it does help prevent us from taking their actions personally.

 # PRACTICE

Self-regulator how-to:

* Pause before responding. Create space to avoid a knee-jerk reaction.
* Take deep breaths into your belly while listening. Feel your belly expand as you inhale and relax as you exhale.
* Become deeply present in your physical body. Feel your feet on the ground, bring awareness to your fingertips.
* Place a hand on your body to help keep you 'in' your physical body. You could place it on your heart, your tummy or press the thumb of one hand into the palm of your other. Consider this your go-to gesture whenever you need to feel safe and grounded.
* Observe what's happening in your emotions and internally name them. *'I'm feeling defensive.'*
* Observe any sensations happening in your physical body. *'My stomach feels tight.'*
* Use an internal mantra to help manage your emotions, such as: *I'm ok with being misunderstood.*
 I can be in this and still be ok.
 Or a self-loving message from your higher self:
 It's ok, hon, I've got you.

As you increase your capacity to self-soothe during conflicts and challenges, you'll find these moments become less stressful. Much of what makes conflict feel so horrible is our feeling that it's dangerous. When we begin to identify our triggers, breathe through the intensity and take it all less personally, it becomes less painful. As we mature in the way we relate, we will begin to rewrite our reactions.

Self-regulation: on the spot

An upside to developing awareness of our triggers is that we can more easily step back and recognise when we are becoming disregulated in an interaction. It's incredibly important to be able to regulate *while* interacting. This will help you to take less things personally, stay clear-headed, avoid becoming defensive and prevent yourself from blowing up or shutting down. The more you practice methods for stabilising yourself, the more stable your interactions – and your relationships – will become.

Self-regulation is the superpower of being able to maintain connection with your loved one during a tough conversation. It's also particularly helpful to use in interactions with someone who hasn't learnt to communicate consciously, or who is intent on fighting dirty.

When all is said and done

What happens after a fight is important. Just because an issue is resolved doesn't mean damage wasn't done along the way. In fact, often the most adverse consequences aren't a result of *what* we were fighting over but *how* we were fighting. How we tend to the collateral damage will make all the difference. Sure, you may want to move on and pretend it never happened, but if you don't process what occurred, it can create distance and take a toll over time, and you also miss out on the lesson.

It's important to take stock of what happened, consider what you did to contribute to the situation and commit to how you would do things differently next time. Zooming out for a moment to acknowledge the circumstances that surrounded the experience will give you more awareness of what to look out for and how to handle it in the future. It's also a game-changer when we take extra steps to end on a warm or loving note. You can do this by taking a moment to acknowledge the lessons learnt, offering positive affirmation and/or reaching out for a hug.

Fighting isn't fun for anyone, but when we choose to be more conscious within our challenges, our endless cycles of conflict are disrupted. Try to address your unresolved disputes in the very best way possible.

Just because you're not fighting doesn't mean it's healthy

Some relationships rarely or never contain challenges or conflict. This may be because the people in them are incredibly compatible, or maybe the relationship is less intimate and contains fewer challenges because the stakes aren't as high. Sometimes, in a long-term relationship, two people have got to know each other well, ironed out the creases, learnt to manage their differences and no longer take things personally.

If you don't experience challenges or conflict in your relationship, that's not necessarily a bad thing. However, you might want to dig a little deeper, just to make sure your situation is really as healthy and harmonious as it appears. Some people may not experience conflict because they're doing everything in their power to avoid it, or they're no longer invested enough to bother with it. If this is the case, your connection may be more wobbly than that of couples that experience robust bouts of slinging matches.

Some questions to ask yourself:
* 'Are there things I want to talk about, but I avoid bringing them up because I'm scared of the reaction?'

* 'Are there underlying resentments that I haven't dealt with?'

* 'Am I avoiding disagreements because I can't be bothered and don't really care anymore?'

* 'Am I scared that the relationship would end if I say how I feel about certain topics?'

If you find that you are naturally just nailing it, good for you! If not, it may be time to confront what's really going on and begin to address the issues. If that's the case for you, go back to the beginning of this chapter and brush up on how to softly and proactively begin a constructive conversation by using 'I' statements.

Final thoughts on relationship challenges

We've been building an emotional lexicon that encompasses new ways of thinking about our behaviour in relationships. Many of us were not brought up with these ideas and rarely are we educated in this way. So go easy on yourself. We've covered a lot of ground and it can take some time (and mistakes made and learnt from) to integrate these practices. Think of this reframing as a huge ship that intends to change direction. It can't just turn in one go. It needs to reset its direction and, bit by bit, it starts to turn. One day, you may find that you've steered yourself in the right direction but be compassionate with yourself along the way. Don't put pressure on yourself to handle your interactions perfectly because now you feel you should know what to do. It takes time to integrate a new way of being.

Start with a small shift in each interaction. Perhaps you start the conversation gently or, mid-disagreement, you manage to self-regulate. Maybe you hold off on a snarky remark that usually gets your partner in a tender spot. Even if the conversation doesn't go perfectly, celebrate where you had a little personal win in the way that you operated.

Maintaining healthy relationships takes consistent practice and commitment. So let's set an intention to create space for our loved ones to grow, to become comfortable with uncomfortable conversations, to let ourselves be amused by our own egos, to be tender with each other's nervous systems, to let go of unhealthy models we've inherited in order to create a new paradigm of connecting.

Conclusion

Let's wrap up with a check-in. Place your hand on your heart –
how are you feeling? Exhilarated, hopeful, determined? Or perhaps
a little heavy, tender or burnt out? It's natural to be exhausted.
Here is where people often give up. But here, and then there, is
where you're going to uncover even more gold. Brave souls will be
rewarded for continuing the work. You're finding new depths by
diving deep.

Carve out space to continue. Life will always feel busy, there will
always be something shiny vying for your attention, yet you and
your people need each other more than ever. By choosing your loved
ones, you're choosing love. So jump on that plane, make time for that
call, come home from work early. You're more likely to regret not
doing these things than doing them.

Our relationships are their own entities. They are destined to be
fluid and as wonderfully unique as our fingerprints. Together, we
have discovered that meaningful relationships call on us to be brave
enough to look at our history, attachments and the agreements we
made early in life. They ask us to rise above our own limitations and
ego. It's an intensely alive process.

As you step out onto your new path, go easy on your loved ones.
They may not understand or have interest in your zest, and that's ok.
People don't change because we tell them to; they change because
they're motivated to. Your internal state will have more influence on
those around you than anything you try to force. Part of your job is
to introduce these new ideas, then let go.

On this path, you recognise that what you seek is right before
you and deep within you. It leads you to an ecstatic existence
where you discover appreciation for the smallest of moments, then
let them open your heart. It's one where you are not only changing
you, you're changing history. This isn't a conclusion, soul seeker.
This is the continuation of your journey. Go well.

Thank You

I would like to acknowledge the Traditional Custodians of the land on which I wrote these words, the Gunditjmara people of the Gadubanud lands. I pay my respects to ancestors and Elders, past and present.

To Alice and the Hardie Grant team. Thank you allowing this dream to become a reality. From that first phone call, Alice, I knew we were going to make some magic together. I'm so grateful to work with a team that I feel so aligned with.

My editor, Libby. Thank you for your enthusiasm and generosity. Your feedback lifted my spirits, put a smile on my face and helped me believe in myself. Your guidance was invaluable.

Thank you to my beautiful friend and writing coach, Jenna. For reading my words, offering your feedback, helping me find my voice and bringing more life to my work. You were there for me when my brain was crashing and my words needed polishing.

Big hugs to my friend and fellow author, Kaylene Langford. Thank you for being by my side, offering your support, sending me wine and having my back.

I owe an enormous debt to the teachers, authors and coaches I've learnt from over the past 25 years. Thank you for paving my way. To Gary Chapman for teaching me to love better when I was 14 years old and found The Five Love Languages. That book set me on a trajectory that had me hungry for knowing - and growing - more.

Huge love to my parents. You taught me the importance of relationships and what it means to have meaningful connections. You encouraged me to be authentically me and for that I'm grateful. Thank you for being there throughout my toughest times, and showing me endless love and support.

To the Power tribe - my siblings and extended family. Thank you for the raucous get-togethers, for all the adventures, friendship, food and laughter we've shared over the years. I love you dearly.

A shout-out to the women in my life. You know who you are. The sisterhood of friends I have collected over the years is amazingly eclectic. But there are common threads that run through these connections; a spirit for adventure, a heart for others, loyalty, kindness, an aversion for small talk and a regular need to put our bare feet on the ground and in the ocean.

An especial thank you to Sezzy, Emsy and Katty. You held me, supported me, checked in on me. You worried for me, laughed at me and are proud of me. Thank you for knowing me so well, and loving what you see.

I'm endlessly thankful to my incredible husband Nootsie. I love you. Thank you for walking this road with me, for supporting this dream and believing in me the whole way. Our relationship has been the testing grounds for much of this work, and I'm eternally grateful for how you consistently rise to grow, learn and apply the lessons we discover together. It was our epic teamwork that made this book possible.

To my darling children, Louie and Zephyr. Thank you for constantly bursting my heart into a million pieces, just by being your authentic selves. You have shown me a love like no other and taught me that the most simple moments in life are where the greatest beauty lies. Life with you is the most wonderful adventure I've ever been on.

And finally, to my sister Sarah. This book is written in loving memory of you. You knew the lessons of these pages without ever needing to learn them. You were born into this world an angel, the kindest person I have ever met. Thank you for showing me unconditional love.

Further Reading

You'll find articles and recommended reading on my website www.emmapower.com. Follow @emma_power for more information on upcoming courses and offerings.

Published in 2021 by Hardie Grant Books, an imprint of Hardie Grant Publishing

Hardie Grant Books (Melbourne)
Building 1, 658 Church Street
Richmond, Victoria 3121

Hardie Grant Books (London)
5th & 6th Floors
52–54 Southwark Street
London SE1 1UN

hardiegrantbooks.com

A catalogue record for this
book is available from the
National Library of Australia

NATIONAL
LIBRARY
OF AUSTRALIA

How to Have Meaningful Relationships
ISBN 9781743796733

10 9 8 7 6 5 4 3 2 1

Commissioning Editor: Alice Hardie-Grant
Editor: Libby Turner
Design Manager: Mietta Yans
Designer: Ngaio Parr
Production Manager: Todd Rechner

Colour reproduction by Splitting Image Colour Studio
Printed in China by Leo Paper Products LTD.

Hardie Grant acknowledges the Traditional Owners of the country on which we work,
the Wurundjeri people of the Kulin nation and the Gadigal people of the Eora nation,
and recognises their continuing connection to the land, waters and culture.
We pay our respects to their Elders past, present and emerging.

Survive the Modern World

Upskill and expand your knowledge with these accessible pocket guides.

Available now

Survive the Modern World

How to *THINK* like an ACTIVIST

Wendy Syfret

Survive the Modern World

How *to start* A SIDE Hustle

Kaylene Langford